SUBURBAN JUNKY

To Ms. Kemp's kids!
Hope you all enjoy my story!

JUDE HASSAN

SUBURBAN JUNKY

FROM HONOR ROLL, TO HEROIN ADDICT

MILL CITY PRESS

PROLOGUE

There are deep secrets that every family holds onto for dear life. Deep, ruining secrets that remain hidden but stay visible enough to remind everyone that the fabric of their family was once tested, nearly destroyed, and will always remain flawed.

Seven years, that's how long I've held onto this secret. Seven years, thirty days, and twenty-one hours, to be exact. The worst part about burying a bunch of painful memories and pretending like they're not there is that they uncover themselves at the worst possible times and in the worst possible ways. I can be sitting at the dinner table with relatives or on my way to see a concert with friends, and outta nowhere, something hits me deep inside, and before I know what's happening to me, I'm swimming in tears. Of course, I can't tell anyone the truth about why I'm crying, so I quickly hide my face and pull myself together and bury the stuff even deeper into my consciousness.

The unbelievable part is that there's really no reason to hide anymore. There's no reason to lie and cover up and pretend. I'm the happiest I've ever been—but that's just it. I deceive because I don't want my happiness to end. I deceive because I'm afraid that if people find out who I really am, they'll never look at me the same again. Naturally, they'll pretend like what I did doesn't matter, but I'll be able to tell just by looking into their eyes that it does. And that's the last thing I want, for people to feel sorry for me or feel like I'm inadequate or troubled or untrustworthy because of a bunch of old painful shit that I did when I was completely different. So I chose to deal with my demons the best way I knew how—by avoiding them altogether.

Then, my wife told me over the phone a while before we got married that if a person gets to be a certain age and doesn't have something to be ashamed of—then something's not right. I forget what we were talking about, but when she said it, I knew it was my chance to come clean. I just couldn't keep lying to her anymore. She deserved better. Although we'd just reconnected after years and years apart and had only been dating for a month at the time, I still wanted her to be the first one to know. She had to know the truth—the truth about what happened to me in high school and why I skipped town and why nobody had heard from me for so long. It was eating at me, that damn secret of mine. I had to tell her.

"I was a heroin addict. No, I *am* a heroin addict," I began. "The whole time we went to school together, I was going into bathrooms between classes and shooting up and stuff. That's why I disappeared. That's why I fell off the face of the Earth, because I was a heroin addict. No, I mean, I *am* one, but I'm better now."

JUDE HASSAN

I paused for a second before continuing. The silence was deafening.

"There's a lot more to it than that, of course, but that's the part that stings most, I guess. If you never wanna talk to me again, I'll understand. I'm sorry I never told you."

I stopped again, and she still said nothing. I started to panic, and I started to sweat, and I wanted to cry, all at the same time. I was sure that I'd lost her. I just knew it.

And that's when she said it.

"I love you."

It was sincere and heartfelt and unexpected and breathtaking. I knew right then and there that it was time to stop running. It was time to uncover my demons and face them head on with everything I had. That's the moment when I finally became, well, free.

CHAPTER 1

An American Family

It became clear to everyone who knew me that my life was coming to an end. My mom was so sure of it that she'd actually started collecting mementos from my room to remember me by—a picture of me on my fifth birthday, a small bag of trimmings from my first haircut, and a pillowcase that held my scent. She kept it all in an old shoebox underneath her bed.

"I wanted to smile when I remembered you in case you left us," she later told me. "I wanted to think back to when things were better, and you were that innocent, adoring son that everyone loved. Now whenever I hear your name, I cry. I just can't help it. You've hurt us so much, Son. But that's not how I want to remember you, so I put this box together to remind me of the good times we had together."

My mother's words pierced through my heart like a jagged shard of glass. Everything had happened so fast and my mind had been numb for so long that I didn't really have a chance to reflect on how much I'd hurt my family. But reflection and redemption are two different things, and the damage from living recklessly had already been done. There was no bringing my father back. There was no brining my best friend back. There was no wiping away the past, period. They're gone forever, and I'm the one who has to live with that guilt. I feel like I deserve it.

I'm not gonna bore you with a bunch of stories from my childhood, except to tell you that before things got really bad, I was actually a pretty normal kid living a pretty normal life. I had an older brother and a younger sister and two perfect parents who lived to serve. My father worked as a drug counselor and social worker in inner city St. Louis, and my mother worked as the director of a daycare/shelter for poverty-stricken mothers in the heart of downtown. My favorite part of the day was when my parents got home from work and the five of us all sat down to dinner in the kitchen of our old wonderful home. My mother was a great cook. We didn't have much money growing up, but she always managed to put together the most amazing dishes, almost every one of them accompanied by rice. Once everyone was fed and all our homework was done, she'd tuck the three of us into bed and read us stories from our favorite Dr. Seuss book. She'd take turns tracing her finger behind our tiny little ears and we'd all fall asleep, one-by-one. I was so happy back then. It didn't matter that we didn't grow up rich or live in a lavish house or anything like that, we were happy and secure, and life was as uncomplicated as it ever would be.

It wasn't until I turned fourteen and we moved out to the suburbs that things took a turn for the worse. My parents had been planning the move for a very long time and they'd been saving up for even longer. I mean, we were leaving for all the right reasons—better schools, fresher air, a bigger house, less crime—the same reasons every other person moves their families outta the city. But mostly, we were leaving because of me. My parents didn't want me going to the local public high school that I would've been forced to attend if we'd stayed. The school had a reputation for ruining kids, at least that's what my dad told me. Up until then, I was a perfect student and a perfect son—just like my parents raised me to be. The worst thing I'd ever done was roll a bunch of tea leaves into a piece of newspaper and nearly burn the house down trying to smoke it, but that was just because I was young and curious—not because I thought I'd get high from the stuff. Nevertheless, my parents decided that it was time to leave and that's exactly what we did. We packed every last worldly possession of ours into a U-Haul truck and headed for greener pastures.

There was no comparison between our old home in the city and our new place in affluent West St. Louis County. It was like every other suburban town outside of a major city, big, green, and fresh. There was a small creek behind our home, a forest of trees directly behind it, and an ice cream parlor a few steps away from the front entrance of our neighborhood. The place seemed so perfect, and almost unreal. It was as if an oil painting had come alive to form this perfect community, far removed from the commotion and insanity of the city. I'd never seen my parents happier than they were on the day we settled into our new surroundings. My father, usually more reserved in his emotions, even started to tear up a little bit as we pulled up to our palace in the woods for the very first time.

But there was something about the place that didn't sit right with me. I distinctly remember getting this awful feeling in the pit of my stomach, like something unavoidable and disastrous was on the verge of happening. Maybe I was just nervous about being the new kid in town, or maybe I was terrified that I'd fall short of my parent's expectations to be a career straight-A student, but whatever it was, the feeling stuck with me. It didn't help that I was set to start high school in a matter of weeks and was being forced to start completely over in the friend department. I had all these preconceived ideas of what high school was gonna be like, and somehow, they all involved getting my head rammed into a toilet bowl, or getting my ass beaten down with a wooden paddle by a gang of unruly seniors. And that wasn't even what scared me. It sounds stupid now when I say it, but my worst fear was eating lunch alone. I was afraid that if people saw me eating alone, they'd assume I was this amazing loser and I'd get picked on for the next four years of my life. To make matters even worse, my brother, the one friend in the world I had left, departed for college a mere week before school began. I was completely on my own.

But it's one thing to imagine being miserable; it's another thing altogether to feel its sting. When freshman year finally came around, all of my conjured-up fears came true. For the entire first half of the year, I ate lunch alone, walked with my head hung low, and talked to hardly anyone. I can't say I got picked on, though, not in the wooden paddle kinda way at least. I was just flat-out ignored, which is almost just as bad. It made me question myself in every way. It made me unconfident and vulnerable, and for the first time ever in my young life, I imagined what it would've been like to be someone else. I imagined what it would've been like to be one of the popular kids—the kids who rarely went to class and smoked cigarettes in the parking lot and always seemed like they had something crazy important going on—the kids who lived in the moment and who everyone wanted to be and know. I mean, who doesn't wanna be popular in high school? Who doesn't wanna be revered and sought after and talked about in all the best ways—the "Zack Morris" of their day? My desire to be "someone" became an unhealthy obsession. I'd go home and look at myself in the mirror and pretend that I was talking to a girl, or at a party surrounded by my high school's social elite. I'd close my eyes before going to bed on Friday nights and imagine what everyone but me was doing, parties and get-togethers and sleepovers and such. I'd never felt so damn lonely and isolated in my life. "Your turn will come," I told myself. "And when it does, everyone will love you and you'll be the life of the party."

But I was a long way off from being popular. I spent most of the year wasting time and staying busy. I joined the football and wrestling teams and flooded my schedule with honors courses and afterschool activities. I was doing so well academically that one of my teachers chose me to be their "STAR" student of the year, and I had to wear this awful gold star on my shirt for an entire day, which I'm positive didn't further my chances of becoming revered and sought after—

not by the kinda people I was hoping for anyway. I should've been proud of that damn star, but I wasn't. In my mind, it just represented three more years of social awkwardness. Call it teenage rebellion, or call it whatever you want. I was simply tired of being ordinary. I wanted more outta life.

Then I met Chase toward the end of the school year, and my life changed forever. He was the backup quarterback for the freshman football squad we both played on. We just sorta started talking one day after practice and things just took off from there. He came off as a really nice kid, but a bit awkward. He had pasty white skin, blue eyes, blond hair, thin eyebrows, a square jaw, and a faded haircut. He was tall, too, maybe six five or so, which made him pretty lanky. He always wore the same blinding white sneakers and baggy black jeans that hung halfway down his legs, forcing him to walk with a weird limp.

Everyone around school called Chase "Ziploc," and I always thought it was because his mom packed his lunch for him in these gallon-sized Ziploc bags, but that just goes to show you how damn naive I was at the time. Really, people called him Ziploc, because he sold tiny Ziploc bags of pot around school, and lots of them. He'd buy pot by the quarter pound from one of the bussed-in kids he'd become close with, flip it the same day to the county kids, and smoke the profits, mostly. He snuck the tiny bags of green stuff around in his sock, or sometimes his girlfriend, Stacy, would hold it for him in her bra. There weren't too many girls like Stacy. She was sweet as all hell, but the chic had a temper like none other. I saw her get into it once with another girl, because according to Stacy, the girl was after her man. The next thing you know, hair's flying all over the freshman hallway and Stacy's beating this poor girl senseless. It was a sad sight, indeed, but that was Stacy for you—sweet, ruthless, and cunning.

Chase definitely didn't slang pot for the money. His parents had enough of that. It was the lifestyle that drove him to do it. Simply put, he loved the attention. Well, that and the extra weed he accumulated after each flip. Lets just say that he never had to spend a dime on the stuff, and he smoked tons. A matter of fact, I don't think I ever saw him white-eyed the whole time I knew him. It made him slower than hell and dumber than a box of rocks, but hey, at least he was popular and had a gorgeous girlfriend hanging off his side. As much as I'd like to, I can't say I didn't envy him. It was all so damn adventurous and off-limits. It gave me an adrenaline rush just thinking about it.

My school had a zero-tolerance policy when it came to drugs, but that did little to stop the stuff from moving up and down the hallways like petty gossip. They were so focused on academics that issues like drug abuse and teenage pregnancy were kicked off to the side and swept under the rug. Sure, if you got caught with anything on school grounds, you were kicked out indefinitely, but they rarely caught anyone to begin with. Most kids who peddled in school were too smart about it to get caught, and even when they did, there was always someone else who'd jump in to take their place. But as much as I'd love to blame my former institution for all my failures in life, that would be too easy and, in a way, untrue. The truth is, looks are awfully deceiving, and although my new surroundings seemed like a pristine place, there was a lot of shit going on behind the scenes that people chose to turn a blind eye to. It wasn't until the whole thing came crashing down and the caskets started to stack up that the blindfolds finally came off.

Now, you'd think my conscience would've kicked in and told me to get as far away from Chase as I could possibly get, but instead, we became even better friends. He introduced me to people, important people, and girls, lots and lots of girls. Suddenly, I wasn't eating lunch alone and I wasn't hanging my head when I walked. Through Chase, I made ten other friends and then twenty more after that. It was all happening so fast. I felt like I owed Chase so much for taking me under his wing and saving me from years of isolation.

I'll never forget the day I was invited to attend my first high school party. It was Friday, and the hallways were buzzing with the usual pre-weekend back-and-forth chatter. I was messing around with my locker between classes when outta nowhere, I heard a familiar voice call out my name.

"Jude. Hey, Jude."

I turned around. It was Chase.

"You gonna ride with me to this party after school?" he asked. "I've got a spot in the car if you wanna go?"

It took all but two seconds for me to respond. I'd imagined that moment in my head for so long, that when it actually happened, I knew exactly what to say.

"Yeah, of course. Who's throwing the party?"

"This chic named Jezebel. I don't know if you know her, but her parents are always outta town, and she's always throwing these insane parties. Anyway, just meet me by my car after sixth period, and we'll head over there. It's the all-black Mercedes up in the top right corner of the parking lot."

"I'll be there, man."

We shook hands, and just like that, I was set to go. I was delirious with excitement, but I tried my best to act cool and uncaring, like it was no big deal. Not only was I going to a party, but also I was going in style. Chase's Mercedes SLK had been a present from his parents on his sixteenth birthday. They had the thing wrapped in this huge red bow and dropped off at school a day after he'd passed his license exam. And there I was still riding the big yellow bus while everyone else was getting cars thrown at them for keeping their GPA's above average. My parents didn't believe in that kinda gift giving. It wasn't that they didn't have the money; they just didn't think it was good for a kid's character to get everything handed to them in life.

"If you work hard, Jude, you can have whatever you want," my dad would always say. "But money doesn't grow on trees. You have to earn it."

That kinda shit made me a bit resentful towards my parents. It made me want whatever it was I was asking for even more, like the pellet gun I'd wanted since I was seven and my parents had always vetoed. When I finally did get that damn pellet gun, I shot it maybe twice before getting bored and putting it away forever.

I phoned my house after football practice and told my mom that I was gonna stay after school to watch the varsity football game and that I'd be home when it was over, around ten or so. I'd never lied to my mother about anything before then. It felt so damn wrong. She told me to have a good time, and she said it in such a way that I almost started crying, because I felt so evil for betraying her. But I didn't have time to feel sorry for myself. Either I was gonna shake it off and move forward with the evening's plans, or I was gonna run home to my mom and sit in my room all weekend like every other weekend prior to that one. Needless to say, I shook it off and met Chase by his car after school let out. It was the first of many very costly mistakes.

He showed up a second later, and we jumped into the car and sped outta the parking lot. It was awkwardly quiet for a moment. I thought of something to say, but nothing came to mind. And then, Chase broke the silence with a bombshell request.

"Hey, can you reach into that glove box and grab out that bag in there?"

"Yeah, of course."

I reached forward and opened up the glove box and blindly grabbed out a massive bag of what I safely assumed was weed. I'd never seen weed before, not ever, until then. There were a bunch of smaller bags inside the bigger bag and then one particularly distinct purple bag shoved in the middle of them all.

"Yeah, that one—the purple sack. Hand that one over here, bro. You gotta see this stuff. They call this shit AK-47. I get it only a couple times a year, but I keep it for my personal stash, ya know. It's too good to sell. It's like three hundred and fifty dollars an ounce."

I handed him the bag, and he opened it up and the smell engulfed the entire car—it smelled like Christmas trees mixed with pinecones and grass clippings.

"How about it, Jude?"

"How about what?" I regretfully asked.

"I usually don't smoke blunts of my good stuff, but it's Friday, and this is our first time smoking together. You do smoke, right?"

I started to shake, but not visibly. I wanted to say no, but I couldn't. I was too concerned with what he'd think of me and what he'd tell everyone if I passed on the opportunity. I felt like I had no other choice but to say "yeah, of course." I'd made my bed, and it was time to lie in it—or however that expression goes.

"Yeah, of course I smoke. It's just been a while."

"Well, there's no better time to start back up than the present," Chase answered, reaching into the bag to grab out a blunt's worth of weed.

He held the steering wheel steady with his knee as he threw a handful of the potent stuff onto a magazine that rested on his lap and split a Dutch Masters cigar right down the middle with the sides of his thumbs. He emptied the tobacco outta the cigar and then sprinkled a good amount of weed onto the empty leaf, tucking the tobacco paper in and around the buds of pot with his fingernails to make a tight cylinder. He finished it off by licking the edges like a dog and drying it off with the flame from a lighter. The process took him a good ten minutes—from start to finish. We drove the rest of the way to the party and pulled over in front of Jezebel's house when we got there. There were at least fifty cars lining both sides of the street and more cars pulling up by the minute.

"We'll smoke, then head inside, alright?" Chase announced, rolling the windows up tight and locking the doors.

"We're gonna smoke with the windows up?"

"Yeah, bro. We're gonna hotbox the hell outta this thing. Trust me—you're gonna wanna inhale as much of this stuff as you can."

He lit the tip of the blunt like a cigar, took a few long puffs, and passed it my way. I was so nervous that I almost puked. At first, I didn't inhale. Then, I took a massive hit and held the smoke inside until it collapsed my lungs and forced me to cough like crazy. Everything in me burned as if my guts had been flooded with kerosene. I coughed a few more times, and then it hit me—hard. It was like the most intense, outta-this-world feeling I'd ever experienced. I felt lightheaded and drained, and then just plain hollow. I didn't like it at first, but the more we smoked, the more it grew on me, and the more confident I got. We kept passing the blunt back and forth until the car was full of smoke and there was nothing left of the thing but a tiny brown roach.

Chase asked me if I was high enough, and I shook my head yes and he laughed. I couldn't really talk, and I was dizzier than all hell. He put the blunt out in a soda can, opened the door, and stumbled outta the car. Clouds of smoke billowed into the open air like a chimney at a coal factory. I opened my door, took one step out onto the pavement, and nearly collapsed. I was tingly, top heavy, and disoriented. There was no doubt that I was high—seriously high.

I got myself together, followed Chase up to the front door of Jezebel's house, and walked in. The house was magnificent—twenty-foot ceilings, marble floors and walls, crystal chandeliers, and museum-like artwork lining every wall.

"*Chase*," the crowd of a hundred or more roared upon our entrance.

We had gotten only five steps away from the front door when I noticed a girl sitting on a rugged-looking leather couch in a room off to the left. She was passed out in her bra with a bottle of something between her legs and a line of vomit running down her chest. She was breathing, but barely.

I wanted to ask Chase about the girl, but he'd already disappeared into the crowd of partygoers. When nobody was looking, I grabbed a blanket off the floor next to her and covered her top half up.

Chase came back a minute later with two beers and a bottle of vodka.

"Is she alright?" I asked, motioning toward the girl.

"Oh, yeah. I'm sure she's okay. That's Jezebel. She always gets like that when she drinks."

"Jezebel? No shit?" I asked, pointing at the house.

"Yeah, bro. But it's cool. Her parents are outta town, remember? We're here to have a good time. Pop that beer open, and I'll grab you another."

"Yeah, alright."

For a kid who grew up in a household where alcohol consumption was considered a sin, popping that beer can open proved to be a pivotal turning point in my life. Of course, I'd just smoked an entire blunt, but for some reason, I had it in my head that alcohol was even worse. Weed was from the earth, but alcohol, well, that was the devil's drink. But if it weren't for weed clouding my better judgment at that very moment, I'm convinced that it would've been a whole lot harder to bring that first sip up to my lips. The stuff was awful. I hated everything about it—the initial taste, the aftertaste, and everything in between. It tasted like I'd imagined urine would—stale and bitter. I finished off the can and then switched over to liquor—vodka and orange juice, rum and coke, and shots of Jägermeister. At that point, I figured that I'd already sinned, so what the hell? Why not make the best of it, right? So, I kept drinking, and I didn't stop drinking until I was seeing double and on the verge of puking. I just remember thinking that no matter how much I drank, it was never enough. It didn't even cross my mind that I had to be home in a couple of hours, sober. All logic and rational thinking had been tossed aside.

I must've introduced myself to fifty people in the first hour of being there. Every time I'd say my name, they'd repeat it back to me, thinking I'd said "Jew" or "Jud" or "Jules." But that's because the music was loud as hell, and the more people drank, the louder everyone else got. It was damn near impossible to carry on a conversation anyway. As the night wore on, kids left and kids came, and some just passed out. A couple fights erupted, and a few things got broken along the way, but judging by everyone's reactions, it didn't seem to be anything outta the ordinary. So I just played it cool and quickly adapted to the disorder as if I'd been to a million other parties and was accustomed to the chaos.

I went outside and took a seat on the patio to get some fresh air and noticed a girl staring at me from across the terrace. It was the first time I'd ever seen her. I couldn't tell if she was just drunk or really into me, but she was beautiful, nevertheless. She had silky black hair, green eyes, bronze skin, and a perfectly proportioned face. She wore heavy eyeliner, red lipstick, and high heels and had her hair up in some kind of a messy ponytail. She casually walked up to me and smiled, showing off her brilliantly white teeth. And then, outta nowhere, she planted her lips on mine, and we kissed for a good minute before a single word was spoken. It was my very first French kiss. I'd always imagined it being a bit more romantic, but regardless, it was incredible and passionate. We talked for a while about school and friends and family and anything else that popped into our heads. It turned out that we went to school together but had never crossed paths.

"Hey, what's your name, by the way?" I asked, right before she disappeared.

"Hailey, my name's Hailey."

And then she was gone, and my vision got blurry, and everything went terribly black.

I woke up an hour later in Chase's car with blood on my hands and on my shirt.

"Dammit, thank God. I didn't know what the hell I was gonna do to get you up," Chase yelled, chuckling.

"What happened?"

"Dude, you passed out and hit your head on the wall. We had to drag you out to the car. You don't remember?"

"No way! I just remember talking to that Hailey girl, and then I got all lightheaded."

"Yeah, well, you were out for a while. I didn't wanna leave you there though—so a bunch of us grabbed you up and put you here."

"Where are we going?"

"I'm taking you home, and then I gotta pick up Stacy."

"What? Home? No way, man. I can't go home, not like this. Look at me, Chase—I'm a mess, man."

"Well, I mean, if I didn't hafta pick up Stacy, then we could go to my house. Are they really gonna be that mad?"

"Chase, my parents don't even drink. They don't do anything, really. My dad's a goddamn drug counselor, and I told my mom I was going to the football game."

I paused for a second.

"Oh my God, what time is it?" I shouted.

"Um, like, two, or so. Why?"

My whole body went numb, and I started to panic. I was so mad at myself for being so dumb. I'd told my mom I would be home around ten, or so. My parents were probably worried sick about me. I wanted to die. My head started pounding so hard that it hurt even when I blinked, I could barely move my neck, and my hands were covered in dried-up blood. I closed my eyes and tried to think of something to tell my parents—something that'd explain my drunken state and late arrival, but I was too messed up to come up with anything believable.

All I remember after that is passing out again and waking up to red and blue lights in the rearview and a cop coming up to the car screaming about how Chase had run a red light. He was so drunk that when the officer asked him for his license and registration, Chase handed them a Jack in the Box receipt and a movie stub instead. Needless to say, he was arrested and charged with driving under the influence, possession of marijuana, and a bunch of other random moving violations.

Four more squad cars showed up in the meantime, and I, too, was handcuffed. They put the things on so tight around my wrists that they cut into my skin and nearly cut off the circulation to my hands. The cop asked me where I lived and then put me into the back of his car and told me that I wasn't under arrest but that he was gonna take me home and have a talk with my parents. My heart sank. I would've much rather been hauled off to jail with Chase or locked up for a month or even beaten severely—anything but face my parents in that shape. I wanted to run away and hide out for a million years, or at least until the anger my parents would soon feel was replaced with worry instead and they welcomed me home with open arms. There was no telling how they were gonna react. I'd never been in trouble before, not even a detention slip at school. I wanted to disappear.

When we reached my house, the officer pulled me outta the car and escorted me up to the front door like a five-year-old. He gave the door a good pounding for about twenty seconds before the porch light turned on and my dad appeared in the doorway. When I saw him, I felt like I'd been punched in the stomach. He stared at me for a second, and then his face became cold and expressionless and I knew that he knew. His eyes got big, and his lips pursed together, and he swung the door open with the might of a thousand men, and before I knew it, he had ahold of my shoulder and I was in the house. He took one whiff of my pot-and alcohol-stained clothes, and it damn near threw him to the ground. The cop walked in behind me, and we all stood around in a weird, awkward circle—all eyes on me. My sister and mom stood at the top of the stairs for a second before my mom realized what was happening and whisked my little sister away to her room.

It was quiet for a second, and then the cop turned to my father and started telling him about what'd happened, and my dad's eyes went from cold to sad and then just plain broken. He finished up by telling me how lucky I was that Chase hadn't killed anyone and how lucky I was to still be alive. He took the cuffs off my wrists and then left, and it was as if he'd never been there.

I turned to my father. He looked like he was preparing to attack me.

"Your mom and I don't deserve this," he started up, clenching his teeth together as he talked. "How could you? After all we've done—how could you? Everything we've taught you growing up about drinking and drugs, and on the very first night you go out, you come home with handcuffs on. Is this fair, Son? Is it?"

I shook my head no.

"Is this what we moved out here for?"

"*No, Dad*—I said no already. I appreciate everything you've done, and I'm sorry this happened, and it won't happen again. It was a mistake."

After that, I rushed upstairs and made it halfway to the bathroom before losing my stomach all over our brand new beige carpet. It was only the first of about ten more trips to the toilet before my vision finally cleared up and the house stopped spinning and I was well enough to get into bed. I don't know if it was the liquor or weed or the two combined that was making me feel so awful, but whatever it was, it sure felt toxic in my body.

I wish I could say it ended there. I wish I could say that I learned from my mistakes and never screwed up again and went off to college and lived happily ever after, but the truth is that it just got worse—a whole lot worse. That night simply served as my indoctrination into the fast-paced world of girls, parties, drugs, and chaos. I was well on my way to high school stardom, and there was no looking back.

CHAPTER 2

HAPPY NEW YEAR

Heroin came into my life on the night that all technology was deemed to fail—Y2K—the New Year's celebration of the century. Chase was throwing a party at his parents' place, and I'd somehow convinced my parents to let me spend the night out. It'd been exactly thirty days since I was brought home in handcuffs and the first time since that night that I was allowed to do anything besides attend school and football practice. My dad sat me down maybe three times during that period to talk to me about drugs, and each time, I assured him that it was a one-time thing and that I'd never drink or get high again. He believed me, for the most part, but I don't know if it was because he actually thought I was telling the truth or because he wanted so desperately to believe me that he willed himself to. It was probably a bit of both.

But instead of putting the brakes on after everything

that'd happened, I turned my decline up a notch and moved right past the experimental phase to the habitual pot-smoking phase of my life. You'd think being grounded would've stopped me from getting high, but it didn't—I just did it at school or before or right after. I'd taken a major liking to pot for a few reasons: I could sneak the stuff around pretty easily, I was making a ton of friends doing it, it was way easier to get than beer or liquor, and, well, I just liked the feeling of being high. Plus, I didn't like drinking much. I mean, having a few drinks here and there was okay, but getting drunk and feeling sick to my stomach didn't really turn out to be my idea of a good time.

I put on my best pair of Seven jeans and Abercrombie hoodie, spiked my hair up like a porcupine, and showed up to Chase's place at about a quarter to nine on New Year's Eve. I greeted his parents who sat in the living room oblivious to the madness around them and let the sound of thumping music and the stench of cigarette and weed smoke guide me to the party in the basement below. I waited a few moments until there was a break in the music and then made my move through the crowd. There were, at least, two hundred people packed into the confined space. The smell was awful, worse than an airport smoking lounge. All the furniture had been moved to one side of the room to open up an area big enough for everyone, but even then, people were squished together like matchsticks. It was a claustrophobic's nightmare.

"Chase! Where the hell is Chase?" I asked a familiar face as I waded through the endless pile of flesh.

"Chase? Um, I think he's in that room back there. I haven't seen him in a while, but he was in there like an hour ago."

"Alright man, thanks."

I was the only person in the place that was sober, and that's only because I was outta weed and had been saving up all week to get an ounce for when the clock struck midnight. And since Chase was the only person I got my stuff from, I had no choice but to find him. I refused to stay sober another minute. Ever since I'd begun smoking pot, the normal lull of life no longer seemed acceptable without THC coursing through my system. It was as if being a pothead had been my calling all along. It summoned me at all hours of the day, like an addiction to crack or something.

The door to the room Chase was supposedly in was closed. I knocked loudly.

"Chase, you in there?"

No answer. The music was so loud that it drowned out my voice. Again, I knocked, and again, no answer. I turned the knob and slowly poked my head through the crack in the door.

The only thing I could make out through the intense smoke in the room was an image of a person sitting slouched over on the floor. Nothing else. I pushed the door open the rest of the way and stumbled into the room as if I'd been pushed in. It was eerily quiet compared to the noise on the other side of the thin wall. The room felt dull and barren. It was as if someone had come in and sucked the life outta it and fed everyone tranquilizers. I'm guessing it was a guest bedroom of some sort, because it was all decked out in bedroom furniture, and there was a king-sized bed square in the middle of the room that took up half the space. The only light in the cramped area came from a couple of black lights that hung loosely from the ceiling like helium balloons. It was just enough light to illuminate one-half of the room and leave the other half completely in the dark. It was like walking into the Twilight Zone.

There were no more than ten, maybe eleven, kids scattered around the tiny room, Chase included. Half of them were dead asleep, and the other half were in this weird, trance-like state, awake but completely unaware. The only person who was up and somewhat white-eyed was a kid I recognized from school—Adrian, I think. He was sitting in the corner sucking nitrous through a whipped cream canister as if it were candy. He had a bag of full canisters on the floor next to his chair and an empty one in his lap. Every time he took a hit of the gas, he'd tilt his head to the right, and his eyes would roll back into his skull and he'd let out a huge sigh—over and over again.

Chase was sitting upright in his bed with a line of drool falling off his chin. I slowly walked up to him and tapped him on the shoulder. He didn't move, so I continued to tap him progressively harder until his eyes opened up and he became aware enough to realize who I was.

"Juuuuudddde!" he shouted, slurping up the drool as if it were water through a straw. "Where have you been, kid?"

He was slurring and talking in this awful monotone voice.

"I've been here, man—trying to find you. It took me a minute to get through the crowd."

"Yeah, bro. I guess word got out about the keg."

"You got a keg? How did you swing that?"

"My parents, of course. I guess they figured I'm gonna drink anyway, so I might as well do it here and not get locked up again."

"Damn, man. I wish I had parents that were that cool. You wouldn't believe the kinda shit I had to tell them to let me outta the house tonight. Anyway, how about that ounce? I'm straight sober, man."

Chase was trying so hard to keep his eyes open.

"Oh, yeah—I got you. I got whatever you need."

He reached into his pocket and pulled out about three or four bags filled with different colored pills.

"What's that?"

"Some crazy good, double-stacked Ecstasy. I got uppers too—like speed or whatever."

He started to reach into his other pocket.

"No, no—I'm good. I'm really just looking to lay back and smoke. Maybe another night though."

"Alright, bro. Alright, but then at least try a line of H before it's all gone."

"H?"

"Yeah, H. You know, H—smack—dope—boy."

"Heroin?" I whispered.

"Yeah, but we don't call it that—we just call it boy. I can't believe you haven't tried this stuff yet. I mean, I don't do it a lot, or anything, but at least every couple of weeks. I'm gonna cut you a line real quick. It's on me, bro."

Before I could even respond, Chase had a plate laid out before him and a tiny baggie of this brown sugar-looking powder laid on top of the plate.

"Alright, there it is—your line," he declared. "Sit down though. You're seriously making me all skittish pacing around like that. You gotta relax, man. Let loose. It's New Years."

Once again, for the second time in as many months, I was faced with another life-changing decision. But this time, the stakes were a whole lot higher. I mean, in all my years alive, I never thought I'd be contemplating doing a line of heroin. Weed was one thing, but heroin? It was the worst of the worst, junkie material. It was the drug that'd always come to mind whenever the words *addict* or *addiction* or *junky* were tossed around . I didn't know what to say. My tongue was tied in all sorts of ways, and I could feel every set of eyes in the room burning a hole in my back like a laser. Peer pressure is an absolute freaking nightmare when it comes right down to it. Where was my D.A.R.E. teacher and that miserable mascot Darren the D.A.R.E. Lion when I really needed them? I tried to think back on all the ways I was taught to "just say no" and all the things my dad had taught me to do when confronted with a situation like the one I was facing, but the words weren't there. I didn't know what to do, what to say, what to do, what to say—my head felt like an exploding watermelon.

I just stared at Chase as he poured a small penny-sized amount of the stuff onto the plate and swirled it around with a razorblade, cutting into the porcelain plate like nails on chalk. He forced the pile around until there were two equal-sized lines parallel to each other in the middle. They appeared so innocent, like little fluffy piles of wheat flour on the family's good china. Yeah, that's what I told myself. *It's just an innocent pile of powder. Everything will be okay. Everything will be okay.*

Everything appeared to be happening in slow motion. Chase rolled up a dollar bill, shoved it halfway up his nose, and sniffed the tiny mound of junk up without hesitation. He held his nose closed for a second, tilted his head back, and snorted like a pig, making sure it'd all gone up into wherever it was heroin went.

I was outta time. It was already my turn. Chase looked up at me with the dollar bill extended out in one hand and the plate in the other. I grabbed both things outta his clammy white hands, wiped the sweat off my forehead, then planted the bill up into my nose. Without thinking, I snorted half of the line up through the paper straw and then the other half a second later. It burned horribly. I immediately felt the powder drip down my throat like paste. I gagged. It tasted and smelled like pungent vinegar. I sat back in my chair, anxious to experience the feeling so many people have died and killed for, the feeling extolled for generations in every facet of popular culture, but the only thing I felt was nauseous. I started to sweat even more than before. Every muscle in my body, from my head to my toes, tingled and then shut down systematically. My thoughts ceased to exist, and nothing but voices and music echoed in the background as I drifted away into hallucination and fantasy. I could hear Chase's voice calling my name from somewhere in the room, but I could barely open my eyes to acknowledge him. I was stuck, stuck in a hole, stuck in my chair, stuck in my body. I gave in and passed out completely.

I slept through the entire night—through the midnight ball drop and the partygoers all around me with their noisemakers and multi-colored confetti bursts. It was five in the morning by the time the drug had finally run its course. The whole evening had been a blur. I rubbed the crap outta my eyes, picked my feet up off the ground, and fell flat on my face the moment my toes touched the carpet. My knees felt like they were made outta rubber, my nose was running like a faucet, and my head was pounding like a damn jackhammer. I felt plain and empty, just plain dead.

I waited a few minutes before I finally had the strength to walk outta the house and stopped when I reached the porch. It was five A.M., and the birds outside were just beginning to make noise. I stood still for a while and watched the sun as it rose above the suburban landscape. I stood and imagined everyone tucked away in their homes sleeping off the mistakes of yesteryear—it made me feel a little better to think about everyone else and their faults. Mostly, though, I was just really confused. I wanted to feel remorseful for what I'd done, but I didn't. I couldn't. I'd made the ultimate sacrifice for the sake of popularity. It was only a couple lines anyway. How much harm could they honestly do? I mean, I was still alive, after all.

CHAPTER 3

THE STAR

A lotta people say that love is the most powerful emotion in the world, but for me, it's always been fear—fear of the unknown, fear of God, fear of death. It's always managed to be the determining factor in whether I do or don't do something. It's always been my guiding light, my conscience, and my saving grace. Once I stopped fearing heroin, there was nothing left to keep me from doing it again. I'd done it, and lived—what was left to be afraid of?

I didn't even make it a week before succumbing to the urge to wanna use again. The stuff had been calling me ever since—it's a miracle that I even made it a week. I told myself that I'd do it one last time and then put everything back together the way it was supposed to be, the way it'd always been. One more time, that's it—just one more time.

I found Chase in the halls and told him that I wanted to "get down" again and that it was my last time doing it, and he said "fine" and "sure" and to meet him behind the cafeteria after last period.

"How much do you want anyway?" he asked.

"I dunno—just like twenty, or whatever."

"So, like a quarter gram?"

"Yeah, sure."

"Alright, well, we hafta go to the north side to get it. I'm fresh out, and unless you wanna get some skimpy, stepped-on bag from someone out here, then that's what we'll hafta do."

"Wait, the north side?"

"Yeah, why? What's wrong with that?"

Suddenly, I wasn't so sure anymore. The north side was where my dad worked. It was where he counseled kids and taught drug-prevention courses and marched in the streets protesting gangs and violence and, of course, drugs in the community. He'd spent countless hours and spilled buckets of sweat and tears in those streets trying to make it a better place, and there I was, his own flesh and blood, considering doing the very thing he'd spent half his life fighting against.

That's not what I told Chase though. God forbid he'd see me in a bad light.

"I mean, the only thing is that I'll hafta skip wrestling practice to go, and I have a match tomorrow," I replied. "You sure there's no other way?"

"No, man—no other way, unless you wanna get ripped off buying it from someone out here. Look, we'll be in and out, I promise. All we gotta do is meet some guy somewhere and we're out, alright? We'll be down there for like five minutes. Then, you can do whatever."

"Seriously?"

"Seriously, man. Just meet me in the hole after school. Alright?"

"The hole?"

"Yeah, you know, where everyone goes and smokes, and stuff? The hole in the woods behind the cafeteria?"

"Oh, yeah. Yeah, alright. I'll be there."

We shook hands, I went to class, and the halls emptied.

The day dragged on for what seemed like forever, and by sixth period, I could barely keep my feet from jumping around under my desk. Ordinarily, sixth period was my favorite fifty-six minutes of the day. It was the one non-accelerated class I was taking and the only hour where I could be myself and not hafta worry about being the "STAR" student. It was also the class that my future wife, Rachel, was in. Rachel was amazing in more ways than one. She had short blonde hair, ocean-blue eyes, high cheekbones, a perfectly shaped nose, a slender body, and a magnificent butt. She was from Tennessee and spoke with this southern accent and said "ma'am" and "sir" and "please" all over the place. Her personality was intoxicating—her laugh, her smile, her cute little belly shirts, and how she didn't seem to give a damn about what everyone else was doing or wearing or saying. She was original. She was unique—and I admired that about her. All I did was care about what other people thought of me. She was stronger than me. She was perfect in all the right ways.

The only crappy part was that I was really into her, but she was stuck on this other guy at the time, and couldn't see it any other way. It's probably a good thing that we'd never dated, because I'm pretty sure I would've screwed something up along the way and she would've hated me for it, but nevertheless, we ended up being just friends, really close friends. We passed notes to each other throughout the day, long notes where I opened up and told her things that I'd never opened up about, like how I'd only kissed one girl in my entire life and how I smoked pot and hated how early my curfew was at home—everything except for the heroin stuff. I wanted to tell her—I really, truly did—but I was convinced she'd look at me differently because of it, and I couldn't risk losing her as a friend. She was my best friend—the only friend I didn't hafta get high with and the only friend I could be myself around. And although we only really hung out at school and she had a boyfriend, it still meant the world to me that she gave me the time of day.

The moment sixth hour ended, I ran to where Chase and I planned to meet, sat on the dirt against a tree in the hole, and waited. I don't know why, but I started thinking about my dad—how we'd once built an entire playground together outta nothing but scrap pieces of wood, and how I used to cry every time he dropped me off at daycare, and how he'd take the five of us camping every year, even though fishing and pitching a tent wasn't really his thing. And then I came home in handcuffs, and things hadn't been the same since. Except for the awkward drug talks we had right after it happened, we really hadn't exchanged words with one another—not even a "hello" or a "goodbye" while passing. It was as if we'd become strangers overnight, and the worst part about it all was that I was too preoccupied to care.

Chase stumbled to the meeting spot a minute later with a skeleton-looking kid by his side named Markus. I didn't know Markus personally, but I'd seen pictures of him in the high school yearbook from the year before when he was a freshman—his only year at the school before dropping out to pursue a full-time career shooting dope. The poor kid was horrifically ugly—thinning black hair, half-shaven eyebrows, cigarette-stained teeth, elfish ears, a devilish grin, and scabs that ran up and down the surface of his cheeks—a grotesque consequence of his own dope-induced cutting habit. He'd get so high that he'd sit in front of the mirror for hours and claw blackheads outta his face until he was bleeding like a stuck pig. He said it was a nervous tick, but everyone knew it was some weird manifestation of his extreme drug use.

Being seen with Markus was like being seen with a needle in your arm or a straw in your nose. There was one reason, and one reason only, to hang with him, and that was to get high. So when Chase showed up with him by his side, I was less than enthused.

I pulled Chase aside and asked him why Markus had to go, and he said it was because Markus knew all the right people and could get the stuff at the cheapest possible price.

"Trust me, Jude, you want him to come. I don't know anybody down there, and it's not the kinda place you wanna go without knowing someone. I'll introduce you guys, and then we'll head out, alright?"

"Fine, whatever you say, man."

Chase hobbled over to Markus, whispered something into his ear, and then turned to me.

"Jude, this is Markus. Markus, this is Jude. Now, let's go before it gets dark."

"Yeah, Shorty said he had to pick up his kids from school, so we really need to get down there," Markus said, staring down at his phone to check the time.

"Then what are we waiting for? Let's go," Chase responded. "My car's just right over here."

"Alright, but can we go around the long way?" I broke in. "I don't want Coach seeing me. I'm supposed to be in practice right now."

"Yeah, sure." Chase answered.

We walked around the entire school, and sure enough, I ran into my wresting coach. It was as if God kept trying to give me chances to turn it all around, but I ignored His signs every time. Coach looked at Markus, then looked at Chase, and then shot me an awful look of disapproval. He walked up to within an inch of me and pulled me aside.

"So I assume you have an excuse for not being on the mat with the rest of the guys right now, right?" he asked.

"Yeah, Coach. I don't feel so great. Chase is gonna give me a ride home so I can rest up. That's all."

"I hope so, Jude. I'm gonna give you the benefit of the doubt here. You've always been a great kid—don't go screwing it up. Get some rest."

"Yes, sir. You don't hafta worry about me. You know I wouldn't do anything that you wouldn't approve of."

"Okay, enough said. Rest up. We have a meet tomorrow."

"Yes, sir."

It was a forty-minute drive from West St. Louis County to the north side of the city, sometimes an hour, depending on traffic. There were three highways, a dozen main roads, and about a hundred, or so, traffic lights separating the sticks from the concrete jungle. I sat apprehensive in the back seat the entire time while Chase and Markus jumped around like two kids on their way to Six Flags up front. Chase lit a blunt halfway through the ride and passed it around to burn time.

About ten minutes out, Markus phoned the connect, Shorty, to let him know we were close.

"Alright, I need that cash from everyone," he announced after hanging up. "He wants to meet at the Amoco over on Kingshighway and Natural Bridge. He said wait by the gas pump and he'll pull up and then to follow him or whatever."

I reached in my pocket and threw my twenty to Markus. Chase did the same. We pulled into the gas station a minute later and parked next to a broken pump. There was no doubt that we'd arrived at our destination—north city. Even with the windows up, the smell of exhaust fumes from the packed city streets was almost too much to bear. A car pulled up to us almost immediately after we pulled in—a convertible old-school Cutlass with the music turned up so loud that it shook the ground beneath us, but it wasn't Shorty. Shorty didn't come for a while, and in the meantime, we just sat there like idiots while everyone in the place stared at us with suspicious eyes. I mean, we were parked next to a broken gas pump for God's sake, and our skin color—well—not to be politically incorrect or anything, but it didn't exactly fit in.

I started thinking about my dad again, how he was probably just getting outta work a few blocks away, and what the chances were that he'd pull into the exact gas station we were at. Actually, the chances were pretty damn good. It was the last service station on the right before the highway entrance ramp, and the biggest one at that. If he didn't pull in, he'd definitely be driving right by us. The seriousness of the situation I'd gotten myself into was becoming all too much to stomach. I closed my eyes as tight as I could squeeze them and tried to will myself to sleep. Impossible. My adrenaline was fired up. I lay down in the backseat and began taking deep breaths of the car's musty, pot-laden air. All I could do was sit and wait for whatever happened next—sit, wait, and pray that everything would go as planned.

"We've got a minute before Shorty gets here," Markus announced as he began to exit the car. "I'm gonna run across the street to Walgreens and grab some syringes and pull a quick lick. I'll be back in a sec."

"A lick?" Chase asked.

"Yeah, I'm gonna heist their asses. You'll see."

Markus slammed the door and vanished into the pool of cars flooding the intersection. Chase turned the music up as loud as it would go.

"Chase!" I shouted over the music. "*Chase!*"

"What's up?" he finally answered back, muting the stereo.

"Did I just hear what I think I heard?"

"What do you mean?"

"Syringes? He's grabbing syringes? I hope he doesn't think I'm shooting that shit up my arm?"

"No, man—it's for him. That's how he gets high. He's been doing this stuff for about two years, you know? You wouldn't believe half the stuff that kid's done to fix."

"What do you mean? Like what kinda stuff?"

Chase paused for a moment before answering.

"Well, would you believe me if I told you that he got his

own cousin hooked on dope and then tried to get her to sleep with the dope man for a gram?"

"You're joking, right?"

"Nope. I wish I was, man. That kid would sell his own mother for a shot. I know for a fact that he's offered his own services to Shorty, if you know what I mean."

"Hold on—what?"

"Yeah, bro. I dated this girl who used to get dope with Markus. Whenever he got high, he'd spill his heart out to this chic. She told me everything. She said that Markus got so desperate one night that he offered to hook Shorty up with whatever he wanted for a tenth of tar."

"*Oh my God!* Like, have sex with him? Jesus, did he do it?"

"Hell no, bro. Shorty pulled a gun on him and damn near shot him just for suggesting it. Could you imagine?"

"Wow. I just don't even know what to say."

I was in disbelief. I tried to imagine the desperation Markus must've felt when he did those awful things, but it wasn't even worth the effort. I simply couldn't put myself in his shoes, not yet at least.

"Ya, well, I've seen him dope sick and it's not pretty. It's beyond hard to watch. He got so sick one time that he shot up Robitussin. The kid's just out there, man."

"Damn, now I kinda feel bad for him."

"Feel bad? Why? It's on him. Believe me, he could clean up if he really wanted to. He's got parents who love him and the whole nine."

"I know, but he just looks lost. That's all I'm saying."

"Yeah, well, he's the one who chose to let this shit take over his life. I mean, look at me. I like to get high, but I can maintain. I know when to stop. That's the difference between him and me."

I didn't say another word after that. I was done hearing about Markus and his miserable existence. It was hard to hear, much less imagine happening to someone. Chase turned the music back up and lit a cigarette without bothering to open a window. I was getting more nauseous by the minute. I jumped outta the car to soak up a few breaths of fresh air, and started slowly washing the windows on Chase's car with one of the squeegees attached to the gas pump to burn time. Five minutes passed, then ten, and another fifteen. After twenty minutes, Markus reappeared with a plastic shopping bag in his hand. I jumped into the car right behind him.

"Goddamn pharmacists!" he shouted. "I hate how they always act like they're not gonna sell you needles when they know damn well that they are. At least I'm using clean needles for God's sake. Whatever, at least I got a hundred dollars off 'em."

"How?" Chase broke in. "You're not even making sense."

"All in a day's work, bro. All in a day's work. How the hell else do you think I get my dope money together? This place and that home repair store off the highway—they all do it."

Chase put his hands up in the air.

"Do what?"

"You gotta work up the nerve to do it, but it's easy once you do," Markus explained. "I just grab receipts from outta the trash right outside the door, run into the store, grab whatever's on the receipt, and return it for cash. Well, it hasta be a cash receipt, and you wanna find something that's worth more than a few dollars, but if you've done it as many times as I have, you know what to look for. For me, it's worth the risk."

Chase glanced at me in the rearview mirror with a huge grin on his face, and we both started laughing hysterically.

"What the hell are y'all laughing at?" Markus asked, irritably.

"You, dammit. You're digging through trash cans now?" Chase shot back.

"Whatever, man. I'm doing whatever it takes. You'll see what I'm saying when you get to where I am—hold on— everyone shut up. My phone's ringing."

It was Shorty, finally.

"Alright Chase, he's about to pull in," Markus announced after hanging up the phone. "Just follow him when he passes us, and we'll stop somewhere. I got the money, right?"

"Yeah, we gave it to you before you left," I answered.

"Alright, here it is."

A second later, I could see someone pull up next to us outta the corner of my eye in a black Cadillac Escalade with chrome wheels as big our car. He drove past us, stuck his arm out the window, and waved us along.

"Follow him, Chase. Follow him. He wants us to follow him."

"Markus, I got it. Chill out. I'm not an idiot. You said follow him like seven times already."

We pulled away from the gas pump and jumped directly behind the all-black SUV. The truck was packed with people, but the tint on the windows was so dark that it was impossible to make out anything but a bunch of blurry objects. We whipped through a neighboring block, making ten or so turns to make sure nobody was following us, before pulling into an alley behind a liquor store. Shorty stopped, stuck his arm out again, and waved us alongside him. We pulled up, and Markus quickly tossed the money through the Escalade's open window. Shorty, in turn, tossed a tied-off baggie filled with black goop back to Markus. The transaction was done within seconds. No hello. No goodbye. We sped off.

It was almost six when we got back to Chase's place. I had exactly thirty minutes to get high, get home, and get settled into my room before my parents got home from work. We filed outta the car and into the house through the basement door. Chase ran upstairs for a second and stormed back down with a plate and spoon. Markus pulled out the dope and threw us each our share, and I threw Chase mine. I didn't know the first thing about breaking out lines or whipping the stuff into powder. The concept of "whipping" didn't even make sense to me. You had this awful-smelling black tar crap that you churned into powder using sleeping pills and a spoon. Black tar is the crudest of all heroin types. It looks exactly as it sounds, like a ball of gooey tar that sticks to everything and melts to your fingers the moment you touch it. The idea of turning it into powder seemed impossible.

But Chase got right to work putting our half of the stuff together as Markus pulled off his belt and removed a fresh needle from his pocket.

"Jude, I'm just gonna whip up your half with mine, break out a line for each of us, and then we'll split the powder. You can take the stuff home or whatever. Alright?"

"Yeah, sounds good, Chase. I just gotta get home."

"Okay, it'll be quick. Two seconds."

It was like watching an orchestra perform a piece they'd practiced for years. Chase ground the powder around on the plate with a spoon until it had the consistency of flour and then cut two lines out with a razor blade. Meanwhile, Markus cooked his portion up in an old blackened spoon. Once it'd liquefied, he sucked every last drop of the brown poison into his syringe and tied his arm off with a belt. He swung his arm around like a monkey until it was bulging with veins and his skin was purple and pale. The needle went into his arm like a hot knife sliding through butter—push and release. He let loose on the belt and closed his eyes as blood from the entrance wound trickled down his fingers.

"Damnnnnnnn," he sighed, in a steadily lowering voice. "Woowwwwww."

I sat speechless. Everything in him went limp, and he collapsed onto the floor with blood still painting his arm.

"What the hell? Markus, you alright?" I asked, peering into his eyes as I bent over him.

He appeared lifeless, as if all the light had been removed from his spirit.

"Yeahhhh, brooo. Yeahhhh, I'm alright."

I quickly turned my attention back to Chase, trying my best to hurry him along.

"You almost done, man? I gotta get home."

"Yeah, I'm done. Get over here."

I walked over to him.

"My pile, your pile, your line, my line. Equal, right?" he asked.

"Yeah, looks equal enough."

He handed me a straw, and I cleared my nose and snorted

the thick line up my right nostril, every bit of it. I shoveled my mound of dope into an empty cigarette wrapper with my school ID card and threw it in my sock. It hit me pretty quick—the burn in my nose, the drip down my throat, and lastly, the warmth in my stomach and then all over my body.

I lit a cigarette, said goodbye to Markus and Chase, ran outside, and began the ten-minute walk home. All I could think about was crawling under the covers of my bed and spending the night sniffing lines in my room. Maybe then I could finally relax and find some enjoyment in the high I'd worked so hard to get.

I got to within line sight of my house when the dizziness took over and I was forced onto the sidewalk like a sack of potatoes. I stuck my hand down my throat as far as it would go until damn near everything in my stomach was on the grass in front of me—breakfast and all. I wiped the puke off my mouth and rushed the rest of the way to my house.

I made it home just a few minutes before my parents. I had to move fast. I jetted upstairs to my room and got right to work emptying the contents of my cigarette wrapper onto a plate and drawing out every last speck of the stuff into five good lines. Before I began, I told myself what I'd told myself from the very beginning, that it was my very last time doing heroin and I'd fix things once I was done.

I sniffed the first line and then another and another until it was all gone. I tilted my head back against my pillow. The powder melted in my nostrils and drained down my throat. Everything went numb—my senses, emotions, and body—the drug paralyzed me. The overpowering feeling of euphoria sent tears to my eyes as I lay and stared at the ceiling. My eyelids became heavier and heavier until they finally shut. Everything became silent. Absolute silence.

My parents came home right as I finished up. I could hear someone walk up the steps, but I couldn't move. I was in a daze. I just remember being awake but having these intense dreams that were so real that I could almost touch them. My mom came into my room to check on me and saw me lying there with my eyes closed and assumed that I was asleep. She bent over me and gave me a kiss on the forehead.

"Jude?" she whispered softly. "Jude?"

I slowly opened my eyes.

"Hey, Mom."

"Is everything okay, Son?"

"Yeah, I'm fine. I just felt a little sick after practice. Coach worked us really hard."

"Okay, well I made dinner if you want to eat. I can make you a plate?"

"No, that's okay. If I get hungry, I'll come grab some."

"You sure you're okay, Son?"

My mom knew something wasn't right—I could see her pupil's circle around the whites in her eyes as every thought but the right one popped into her head.

"I promise you. I'm okay—just nauseous. Other than that, things couldn't be better."

She paused for a moment.

"Okay—well you can tell me anything. You know that, right? I'm always here for you."

"I know, Mom. I know I can."

I was sure she knew something. I was sure of it. She stared into my eyes and then around my room and back to my eyes.

My heart stopped for a second.

"Well, I'll let you rest. I love you, Son."

"Love you too, Mom."

She gave me another kiss and left, and I faded right back into paralysis.

CHAPTER 4

Mr. Popular

Contrary to what a lotta people think, it actually takes a decent amount of time before you become physically addicted to heroin—like weeks or a couple months, depending on how much you're using. It's your brain that screws you in the beginning. You do the stuff once, and all of a sudden, it's not so scary anymore. It goes from being HEROIN to just another drug. Then, you do it again and start to actually like it. You begin to revel in the euphoric rush that the powder gives you as it drips down your throat and numbs your brain and body and everything in between. You tell yourself that you're only gonna do it "one last time" and then "one last time," and you mean it every time, but then you can't stop, and you lose hope and don't care anymore. That's usually how it plays out anyway.

Going from pot to heroin in a matter of months had me feeling invincible. Nothing seemed off limits anymore, and there was still so much left to discover. Every day at school, someone had a new pill or powder or plant to try out—hash resin and opium sprinkled over homegrown marijuana, ecstasy and pure MDMA, acid papers and mushroom caps and liquid LSD, cocaine and heroin powder, oxycontin and Adderall, Vicodin and Percocet, and on and on and on. There wasn't a drug you couldn't get roaming the hallways at my school—except maybe meth and crack. I don't know anyone who got down on that shit. I guess they were just considered too grimy and low class to appeal to the high-end clientele in my suburban environment. Although that's what everyone thought about heroin before it became more accessible to teenagers than alcohol, and perhaps even cigarettes. It's scary when you really think about it—how quickly a trend can take over a group of people, even when the trend is something detrimental like a heroin or coke habit. It's nothing new, though, and I'll be the first to acknowledge how easy it is to fall in line when a little pressure is applied. I used to think that peer pressure was just something that adults made up to bother kids with, until I had a plate with a bunch of lines shoved in my face and I discarded my morals faster than a politician running for president.

Kids literally planned parties around what drugs were available and whose parents were outta town on that particular weekend. Now to be clear, not everyone partied—it was about half and half, and even less than that got high—but when you have two thousand students in a single school, even a small percentage can be a lot. On paper, though, you'd never have known what percentage of people partied and what didn't. You see, most kids could pull themselves up by the bootstraps and put down the joint or beer or whatever whenever it was time to make the grade. Girls were most amazing in that way—they'd put on a pretty face and wipe away the transgressions of their prior Fridays and Saturdays with the simple swipe of a pen on a Monday test. Maybe they were just smarter, I dunno, but they sure as hell had it down to a science.

And meanwhile, my grades were slipping fast. I wasn't as strong-willed as everyone else, I guess. I couldn't stop partying just because it was time to make the grade and focus in on the years ahead, college in particular. College seemed so far off at the time—so freaking insignificant. What mattered was the present—the parties and girls and drugs. By sophomore year, my A's and B's had turned into C's, and my grade point average had sunk to an all-time low. There was nothing gradual about it, either. One week, I was fine, and the next, I wasn't. It was as if I'd woken up one day and simply stopped caring—stopped studying, stopped doing homework, and stopped wanting to do well in school. The more drugs I did, the emptier I felt, and the emptier I felt—the less I went to class and the more I snuck outta the house and the easier and easier it became to lie. My coaches and teachers did their best to bring me back from the dark path I'd stumbled onto, to no avail. To be quite honest, I don't think even they knew what to do.

When it came to my parents, though—I just kept them in the dark. It wasn't as hard as you might think. I'd skip practice and run home to intercept and alter progress reports whenever they were sent out, forge my parents' signatures on disciplinary notices that I'd begun racking up by the dozen, and erase phone messages from teachers and principals about my attendance and poor performance in class. The phone would ring, and I'd run to the thing like a bat outta hell, but usually, I just turned the ringer off altogether. I knew that it was inevitable that a call would slip through or a letter would make its way into their hands, but the inevitable wasn't something I spent much time thinking about. Like I said, it was all about the present—the then, the now, the immediate.

Things only got worse from then on. One by one, everything I'd built up to since I was a baby in my mother's arms fell by the wayside. As soon as my grades turned to crap, I was deemed ineligible to play sports. I was taken outta all honors courses, placed in less challenging classes, and more or less, forced outta all afterschool activities. As with everything else, I didn't tell my parents what'd happened but instead used the extra time after school to pick up where I'd left off with heroin. Smoking pot was no longer doing it for me—the same empty high over and over and over again—and outta every drug I'd experimented with, heroin was the one I thought about most. After that second time using alone in my room, I hadn't gone a single day without thinking about it. The high was unforgettable, indescribable. It was as if the world had stopped for those few moments of ecstasy and every good feeling that'd ever existed since the beginning of time overtook my mind and body and soul and I was at peace—at peace without a single thought or a single discomfort—nothing but echoes.

I know I'd told myself that it was my last time ever touching the drug, but that was all B.S. for what it's worth. I just said that stuff to make myself feel better for doing it again—to justify the process. I mean, I guess I really did believe I'd be able to do it one last time, but the moment I did it that second time, there was no going back. Not ever. The feeling would stay with me forever.

Heroin went from being a one-and two-time thing, to a weekly thing, and then an every-chance-I-could-get-my-hands-on-it thing. Once summer vacation rolled around, we were doing it almost every day. There were five of us in the group—Chase, Markus, Davey, Tommy, and myself. I knew Davey and Tommy from school but hadn't really become friends with either of them until Chase introduced us to one another over a plate of powder. Davey and Tommy were stepbrothers, but looked more like brothers, although Tommy was heavyset and Davey was skinnier than a rail. They both had shaggy blond hair and droopy blue eyes, uneven eyebrows, and square jaws. They dressed really preppy-like and spoke proper English and came from a wealthy home. They reminded me a lot of myself, in that they seemed to be genuinely well intentioned but confused as all hell and stuck in the mud. They'd stumbled onto the drug just as I had—peer pressure and a weak backbone mixed in with a series of bad decisions. That was how they'd started using anyway. It wasn't until Tommy and I were alone one day that he got real with me and told me the actual reason behind their habit.

"It's the only time of the day that I'm not thinking about how crappy things are at home," he began. "My parents are so occupied with their little divorce and custody bullshit that I don't even think they care. And then I find out that my dad touched my sister when she was small. It just sucks—Davey and I are just so in the middle. My dad thinks he can just keep throwing money our way and everything will be okay. No. It's not okay. He freaking touched my sister, and honestly, I wanna kill the bastard."

I don't know what it is about me that makes people wanna open up and tell me their darkest secrets, but it seems to happen a lot. Ultimately, I think it just comes down to the fact that I'm an okay listener and a great secret keeper, which is all people want anyway—someone who'll listen to them unload without ever speaking a word of it. I've always been trustworthy with stuff like that.

I felt really bad for Tommy and Davey. I felt like they were too good to be sitting in a basement with the rest of us snorting dope. Me, well, I felt like I deserved the casual screw-up. I'd been good my whole damn life. It was my turn to be a little reckless and foolish. But then again, I never thought things would turn out the way they did. I'll never understand how I was able to trick myself into believing that I could push the boundaries so far, and never get pushed back. Maybe I was just too spoiled and sheltered to believe that something awful could ever happen to me. I knew that my parents would always be there to bail me outta trouble, but the kind of trouble I was headed for didn't allow second chances. It stuck with you forever like an ugly tattoo or an awful scar on the most visible part of your body. The trouble I was headed for was everlasting.

Whenever it was decided that we'd go downtown, we'd all scrape up as much money as we could and throw down on the same bag—then split it five ways. The more we went down, the more I became comfortable with meeting drug dealers in dangerous places and the more of an adventure it became for all of us, I think. We'd ride the highways deep into the early morning hours, sharing stories and blunts and plates of H, until we were falling down wasted and half-dead. It was glamorous in an odd way. The ritual of copping the stuff became as addictive as the heroin itself—it was dark and mysterious and unknown and forbidden.

The more money we brought Shorty, the nicer he got. He grew to know each of us on a personal level and began treating us as such. He started letting us into his home and into his world, which wasn't as desirable as I'd imagined it being. His house was normal, and although he had ten cars, they were all Chryslers and Hondas and Chevys and Dodges—no Bentleys or Beamers or super sports cars. He had a bunch of kids and a boatload of bills and a wife who was decent looking and held a regular job. They put everything of value in her name, so on paper, he appeared broke—but in reality, he had a freezer full of cash at home and even more money stashed away at different spots throughout the city.

"It's the guys who wanna have everything who end up getting popped in this game," he explained to us once. "I don't need all that flashy crap to be respected—everyone who needs to respect me does, and you can ask anyone who I am and they'll tell you that I'm the last person you wanna mess with. That's good enough for me."

Shorty was the type of guy who would laugh with you and even throw you a little extra dope if you were loyal to him, but he made sure we knew that he meant business. If you went to him short on cash or if you suspected you were going to someone else to get your stuff, he'd leave you hanging for hours and hours, or he wouldn't come through at all. He'd tell you to come downtown, but then he wouldn't show, and you'd be left high and dry with a broken spirit. Then, the next day, you'd see him and he'd pretend like nothing ever happened or he'd throw you some lie about this and that with a joke in between, and all you could do was laugh and play nice. Shorty wasn't a friend. He didn't trust us or care about us or make conversation because he wanted to be our friend—he wanted to make money. And that's all he cared about.

As the months passed, money started getting tighter. We were using more to keep up with our growing demand to get higher, and twenty-dollar bills weren't cutting it anymore. A gram of tar went for about eighty, sometimes sixty, dollars, and a gram was barely enough for the five of us. Our tolerance to the drug was building, and each time, we had to do more to achieve the same high as before.

Now, let me be clear when I say this—I hated needles. There's nothing that I hated more than the prick of a needle popping into my skin. I'd always told myself that I'd never stick a needle into my vein no matter what transpired, but I was at a crossroads with the drug. Anyone who does heroin for a decent amount of time eventually gets there. In the ultimate chase for the ultimate high—the high I hadn't experienced in a very long time—I was willing to turn to the needle to once again reach that plateau. It's a story as old as time. You spend the rest of your days as a dope user chasing your first or second high or whatever high was most memorable, but you never get it. So you evolve and resort to doing riskier stuff to reach that place up in the stars, like shooting up in your jugular vein or squirting a dose of H up your rectum. Nothing was off limits when it came to the things a person would do to fix.

So, naturally, I approached the only person I knew who shot up—Markus—and he was more than elated to oblige me. I don't know if his excitement came from some sadistic place within him that liked seeing people screw their lives away or if it was because he actually thought he was doing a good thing for me—but, either way, I threw him ten dollars for needles, and we agreed on doing it that night.

We'd all just left a party after finishing off a gallon jug of Bacardi rum and were equally drunk when we hopped into the car and began our usual downtown run. I had a fifty-dollar bill in my pocket, which I'd taken outta my dad's wallet before sneaking out way earlier in the night. Usually, I just used my allowance money to get by, but on that night, I wanted more than the ordinary—at least enough to last me a few nights.

Actually, Davey and Tommy had stayed behind, so it was only the three of us—Chase, Markus, and myself. It was better that way though; the less people in the car, the better and less suspicious—especially at two in the morning when every other car on the road was a cop.

On the drive down, Chase nearly killed us at least ten times due to his drunken condition. By the grace of God, however, we somehow made it to our destination right off the highway. Shorty ran outside half-asleep, we exchanged goods, and the deed was done in record time.

Instead of heading back to the county to get high, Markus called up an "old friend" of his that lived around the corner from where we'd met Shorty and convinced him to let us fix over at his place. Markus said he wanted to be in a room with good light, so he could see my veins well enough to hit them.

I was irritated that he'd remembered our earlier conversation about pricking me with a needle. I was kinda hoping he'd forgotten, so I could just stop thinking about it and let the whole idea slide by. But he hadn't, of course. His brain was mush when it came to everything else, but when it came to drugs, his memory was as sharp as the best of them.

The street his friend lived on was in one of the worst areas I'd ever been to. There were more vacant lots in the neighborhood than there were buildings and more abandoned or boarded-up homes than there were occupied ones. The place seemed forgotten, not even worthy of trash removal or a police presence. You could feel the emptiness in the air. It was dark and unnerving.

When we pulled up, I forced myself outta the car, and the three of us hurried up to the front of the building. Markus's friend buzzed us through the front door, and we walked in. The place reeked of body odor and stale cigarette smoke. It looked like an abandoned hotel from the early 1900s—completely outdated and torn to shreds. The wallpaper was half-gone, and the mailboxes were all empty and open. Our feet echoed off the walls as we tiptoed along the filthy linoleum floor with only a few flickering lights to help guide our way. I followed Chase, and Chase followed Markus through a series of dark hallways to a broken elevator.

"We gotta take the steps," Markus whispered, as if we weren't completely alone.

Chase turned to me and tried to crack a smile, but I could tell he was just as hesitant as I was. Seventeen flights of stairs—that's how many we had to walk up to get to the place—and the hallway upstairs was even darker and emptier than the entrance downstairs. It reminded me of that movie *The Shining*, except it was even creepier.

"707. This is it," Markus announced as he knocked on the aluminum door with the side of his hand.

"Bill, it's me—Markus. Open up."

The door creaked open.

"Markus?" an eerie voice called through the small opening.

"Yeah, Bill—it's me. You said it was okay to come by?"

"Yeah, of course, man. Come on in. It's just been a while, ya know."

"At least a year or two," Markus responded.

Markus's friend—Bill—opened the door the rest of the way and summoned us in. I still couldn't see his face. It was way too dark, and he turned around before I could make my way inside the one-room disaster. Markus closed and locked the door behind us—six deadbolts to be exact.

The room was bare—no furniture, no clothes, no food—just bare. The air was so heavily polluted with stench that the taste of feces and urine and body odor seeped into your mouth and made you instantly sick. The three of us took a seat on the floor next to Bill and some girl, who I assumed was his girlfriend. Bill was naked except for an American flag that he wore around his shoulders like a bathrobe and a piece of rope that held the flag in place around his waist. Every inch of his pale skin was bruised and needle-marked and swollen—from his neck on down to his toes. He had fairly long, stringy hair, green eyes, and a thickly matted beard. The poor guy could barely keep his eyes open or finish a sentence before succumbing to whatever drugs he was on and nodding off. When he closed his eyes, it looked as if he was dead, which

I'm sure he wasn't far off from being. There was nothing left in him, not even a mild sparkle of life or a hint of a soul.

The girl that sat next to Bill was equally bruised-up and ballooned out. Her name was Mandy. Her eyes were heavy, and each bone in her body protruded outta her skin like a malnourished African baby. Mandy's hair was so greasy that it stood up on her head in chunks, and if you looked close enough, you could see little pieces of food and filth mixed into the knotted mess. Her face was saggy, and her skin was baggy, like elastic. Neither she, nor Bill, could've been older than twenty-five, but years of banging dope into their veins had them looking about fifty. It was shocking and sad all at once.

We formed a circle on the floor around an endless pile of needles and charred spoons and candles. Markus tore open a bag of fresh needles and got right to work cooking up. I could smell the vinegar scent of burning heroin. It faintly covered up the foul smell in the room, but only for a second. Chase had already begun whipping his portion up into powder on a plate.

"You sure you wanna do this, Jude?" Markus asked.

"Um, yeah, I guess—as long as it doesn't hurt."

Chase looked at me from across the room, slightly shaking his head as if to warn me.

"Look, I'll do you first. From start to finish, it'll take thirty seconds. Just take off your belt and wrap it around your arm as tight as it'll go," Markus explained. "Shake your arm if you have to; just try and get a vein to bulge out."

"Alright."

I was uneasy, to say the least. I was still kinda drunk from way earlier, and wasn't thinking as clearly as I needed to be. I watched Markus to make sure he put my stuff in a fresh rig and then proceeded to choke off the blood supply in my arm.

Markus slurped the brown liquid into the needle and scooted to within an inch of me.

"Wow, you're gonna be easy, bro. You've got veins for days. Just take a deep breath, and relax," he said, wrapping his clammy hand around my arm.

"Stop messing around. Just tell me when it's done, dammit. Just please hurry up and do it already."

I looked at Chase. He shook his head again, and I closed my eyes tight.

"Okay, Jude. Here goes nothing."

I felt the needle pinch my skin. My eyes were closed as tight as they would go, but I could feel the syringe prodding around in my arm like a needle searching for thread. It made me sick.

"Got it. Don't move, Jude."

He pushed down on the plunger and snapped the needle outta my skin.

"Okay, now loosen the belt slow. Sit back. It's gonna hit you hard—very hard. Just take it in, alright?"

Before the belt was even off my arm, I was on the ground. It hit me—the rush. It hit me so hard that it literally took my breath away and sent me sinking into the ground. My head, my heart, and my body—everything echoed with the intensity of a tornado siren. It felt like I'd snorted a thousand lines of H at the same time. I could feel the dope burn through my veins on its way through my body and to my heart. Then, I passed out. It was too much.

I stopped breathing and turned purple and, a few seconds later, woke up to screaming.

"Jude, wake up. Jude."

I slowly sat up.

"I'm okay. I'm alright. I'm alright. Stop with the screaming already," I mumbled.

"You're okay?" Chase worriedly asked. "You hit the floor and started shaking around like a fish. We thought you were overdosing, kid. Don't ever scare me like that again, dammit. I told you not to give him that much, Markus."

"What? Me? I didn't put but a tiny bit in there. It's just his first time and—"

"Look, I'm alright," I broke in. "I just got real dizzy is all. I'm good now. Stop screaming, and let's get outta here. I gotta be home before my parents find out I'm gone."

"Alright, let's go then," Chase answered back. "I can do my stuff in the car."

We said our goodbyes to Bill and Mandy and headed home. I was a mess—still tipsy from the rum and completely out of it from the H. I was itching so much from the shot that I'd cut into my arms with my fingernails. I lit a cigarette and fell asleep, and the damn thing burned through my jeans and stopped just short of my skin. I was totally incapacitated. Every time I tried to lift my head up to talk, it fell down like a bowling ball. And every time I opened up my mouth—I just bumbled and slobbered all over myself like an old man. So I gave up and passed out.

We got to the county just before dawn. Chase dropped me off at the back entrance to my house, and I carefully snuck in through the basement door and up to my room. I'd become somewhat of an expert at getting in and out undetected. I would spend hours memorizing my parents' sleeping habits and the noises of our home—the creeks in the steps and the squeaks in the doors. Getting caught wasn't an option. It simply couldn't happen, especially since they'd begun sniffing around more than ever. They were completely convinced that something was wrong with me, although they couldn't figure out what. I think they probably just assumed that I was just going through some sorta teenage rebellious phase. They'd even taken me to see a psychiatrist, a friend of my father's, to maybe see if I'd open up to him—but I just lied through my teeth and fed him the same crap that I'd fed my parents: "I'm fine," and "I just want everyone to leave me alone," and "There's nothing wrong with me," and on and on and on. The doctor prescribed me Adderall, thinking that it'd fix everything, but I didn't take a single one. I just sold them at school and spent the profits on junk and weed.

Markus was right—there was no going back after the needle. That one shot washed away whatever hope I had of coming to my senses. I spent the next month of my life learning how to stick myself with precision—in the arm, in the foot, and in the side. I became, in a way, addicted to the feel of a needle. The simple thought of a one cubic-centimeter rig crawling under my skin sent shivers down my spine. I became so used to having a syringe in my arm that I'd shoot up plain water when I didn't have dope just to keep my mind at ease. It was a mental fix.

I never thought I'd ever be okay with needles. As much as I hated them growing up, it just didn't make sense that I could inject myself like it was no big deal. I wasn't even thinking about all the crap I was putting into my body, either. I mean, it could've been poison for all I knew, and in so many ways, it was poison. Overdosing just never crossed my mind. It's just one of those things that you never think will happen to you until it actually does, and by then, it's way too late.

CHAPTER 5

THE GIRL

W hen she came into my life for the second time, it was the first time I'd ever entertained the idea of cleaning up my act. Her name was Hailey—the same Hailey I'd met a year before when I was a sophomore and just getting into the party scene. Of course, that was the same night I hit my head, blacked out, and was brought home in handcuffs because Chase was too drunk to drive. So it kinda seemed fitting that she'd be the one who helped me get it together. I guess there was a part of me that wanted to get clean, but I needed something to value other than drugs. I made her that reason. It proved to be an awful mistake.

Everything about Hailey gleamed, from her jet-black hair and her soft skin to her brilliantly inviting smile and innocent demeanor. Every time I passed her in the hallways at school, I'd get extra loud or walk right in front of her to get her attention. She'd just smile and keep walking, and it drove me crazy that she didn't seem at all interested in me—but it just made me want her even more. I made it my mission to be with her.

It took a while, but I finally gathered up the strength to ask her out, and outta nowhere, she said yes. It was unexpected, to say the least. I'd spent so much time hanging out and getting into drugs that I rarely had a moment to think about properly taking a girl out. I mean, I'd "hooked up" with a few girls here and there at random parties, but those were just flings—one-night stands. The only other person I'd even pondered asking out was Rachel, but she was taken, and I kinda stopped trying after I spilled my heart out to her in a letter and she turned me down. But I wanted a girlfriend, someone I could go steady with—and Hailey seemed like the perfect fit.

I ran home after school to get ready for our date, talked my mom into giving me some money and the car, and tried my best to put heroin outta my mind for the night. I still had a quarter-gram left over from the night before, which I had stashed away in the ceiling tile of my room—along with my needles and spoons and tourniquet. I figured I'd go out clear minded and do one good shot when I got home to celebrate if all went well. That was the plan, at least.

I grabbed some roses from a nearby florist on my way to Hailey's house and showed up with a few minutes to spare. She came outside wearing this strapless silvery sequined dress that crawled up to her knees and made her legs look extraordinary. I blushed when I saw her and handed her the flowers.

"Oh my God—nobody has ever given me flowers before. You're so sweet, Jude. Thanks."

"You're so welcome. You look amazing, Hailey."

"You too," she said, smiling, putting the flowers up to her nose to smell them.

I opened the passenger side door for her like a proper gentleman, got into the driver's seat, and we headed out. She grabbed my hand right tight as I sat down, and we drove in silence the entire ride to dinner. Her tiny fingers sent electricity through my body—it felt so perfect. Everything felt perfect.

We hit it off at dinner and talked like old friends.

"To tell you the truth, I'm a little intimidated by you," she went on to say. "You just have this reputation at school, and I'm just not that kinda girl. All my friends thought I was crazy when I told them we were going out, but I can tell you're a good guy under it all."

"Really? A reputation, huh?"

"Yeah, you know—for smoking pot and partying. Nothing horrible, but my mom works for the District Attorney, so she's really strict about who I go out with."

"I mean, I understand. You don't hafta be intimidated though. I just kinda fell into that whole scene, but it's getting kinda old. I've calmed down a lot since sophomore year."

I was already lying, and we hadn't even made it through our first date—but surely, I couldn't tell her I shot heroin on a regular basis. Especially not after she told me about her mom, and how she wasn't that kinda girl, and all that. I had to reinvent myself. I had to be whoever it was she wanted me to be.

We left dinner and headed to a nearby mini-golf course, and I let her beat me every time. We talked and talked and talked as if time didn't exist and we had our entire lives to get to know one another. I took her home just before ten o'clock, and she gave me a kiss just before getting outta the car. Her lips tasted like strawberries, her skin smelled like vanilla, and her hair smelled like an infusion of apples and peaches and watermelon.

"You know you're the first girl I've ever kissed like that, right?"

"What do you mean?"

"At the party, remember? You came up to me and gave me this amazing kiss?"

She looked down and thought for a moment.

"Oh my God, you're right. I totally forgot about that. It was your first kiss? Really?"

"Yeah, it's kinda embarrassing, huh?"

"No, I think it's really cute. I think it just shows how amazing you are, Jude."

She went on to tell me that she had an amazing time and she couldn't wait to do it again, and I said that I felt the same way. She gave me one last kiss and vanished into her house.

The night couldn't have gone any better. Suddenly, things weren't looking so dark, and I had a reason to look forward to the next day—and the next day after that. This amazing girl had invited me into her life, and it was beautiful and innocent and full of hope. She'd brightened up my world in one night. I smiled the entire way home. I smiled so much that my cheeks began to hurt.

Perhaps, the best part of the evening was that I hadn't thought about heroin at all—not even once—until I got home and the stuff started calling me from the ceiling tiles. I locked my door, grabbed my needle and spoon, and shot up a nice-sized chunk of dope before lying down. I thought of it as my reward for going all night without using. Pretty messed up, huh? But that's how heroin starts to rewire you. It's the evilest of all evils. I didn't know it right then and there, but I couldn't have quit even if I tried. It had me and it wasn't about to let go, especially not for some girl.

The next day at school, I asked Hailey if she wanted to be my girlfriend, and she said yes. It was probably the best day of my life. No, it was the best day of my life. I just remember picking her up and giving her this amazing hug and kiss in the middle of the junior hallway. We looked at each other for a while, and then she headed off to class. I looked upwards, as if looking at God Himself, and I silently thanked Him for giving me a chance to make things right. But I wasn't outta the woods just yet. I had to go straight before Hailey found out who I really was. Maybe one day I could tell her that I shot heroin a bunch of times and we could have a honest conversation about it, but I imagined that would be years down the road. First, I had to get clean.

There was only one problem—I was starting to get dope sick. I didn't know it until later on that week when I tried to go a day without doing the stuff, and couldn't. At first, I thought it was just the flu—sweats and sneezing and chills. It wasn't until I shot up a tiny piece of junk and the symptoms disappeared that I realized that it wasn't the flu but heroin withdrawal. My worst nightmare had come true. I was turning into Markus. I decided that the best thing to do was wean myself off the stuff by doing a little less each time until I was doing nothing at all. And that's what I did. I did a small, watery shot each morning before school and each night before bed. I wasn't getting high, but I wasn't getting sick. Mostly, I wasn't going downtown as much, so I had all the time in the world to spend with Hailey. We spent hours together after school and on the phone and wrote notes to one another all throughout the day. She told me everything, and I told her almost everything. I'd even stopped smoking pot, going to parties, and, for the most part, associating with Chase and the rest of the group. My grades were on the rise, and I'd reinserted myself back into the family dynamic. My parents even gave me my brother's old car, a raggedy Honda Civic that'd been completely wrecked three times and brought back to life by my father. All the ties that I'd worked so hard to sever were fusing back together again as if they'd never been severed to begin with. I was happy. I was really, really happy.

And then, three weeks into our relationship—she found it. We were studying at my house, I fell asleep for a second, and she found the damn thing. All the blood in her face drained, and she turned pale.

"*Jude*, why do you have a needle in your drawer?" she cried out, nudging me on my side with her right hand as she held the needle up with her left. "*Jude*."

I opened my eyes, and my whole body went numb, and I couldn't speak for a second.

"Hailey, I was gonna tell you, but—"

"But what? You were waiting for me to reach in one of your drawers and get stuck like I almost did? I wasn't snooping around, either. I was looking for a pen. Tell me, Jude. Please tell me you're diabetic or there's some rational explanation for all this."

I said nothing. I couldn't think of a lie fast enough. She started crying.

"Please tell me this is not what I think it's for. Please, Jude. I've defended you so much to everyone. Jude, please tell me why you have a needle next to a spoon in your drawer? Please."

I put my hands on her tiny shoulders to calm her down, but she shook them off right away.

"You promise you won't get mad?" I pleaded.

"Jude, *no*. I don't hafta promise anything. You need to come clean with me right now, or I'm gonna be ten times more upset and hurt. You not saying anything kinda says everything."

"*Fine*. Here it is—I've done heroin a few times, *but* I'm done now. I've never been happier in my life, and I want to get clean, so we can be happy together. I'm gonna get clean. I promise. I'm only doing a tiny bit here and there just so I don't get sick. I'm not like a junky or anything. Please, you hafta believe me."

She walked up to me and pulled up my right sleeve, exposing my red, needle-marked arm.

"Dammit, Jude. I really liked you a lot. I thought you were different."

And that was it. She wiped the tears outta her eyes, kissed me one last time, and disappeared.

"But I *am* different, Hailey!" I screamed. "I *am* different! Please, come back!"

But she was gone. We never spoke again after that day. It was over. Our month-long love story had come to an abrupt end. And as if my heart weren't broken enough, she started going out with a friend of mine only a few days later. I'd never felt so much hurt in my life. I felt betrayed like never before. I just remember going into my bathroom at home after finding out about her and my friend and chain-smoking an entire pack of cigarettes just to calm myself down. When I finally stopped shaking, I cooked up an enormous shot of dope and injected the hot liquid deep into my arm. It was the most I'd ever done in a single dose. I let loose on the belt and was overtaken by the rush. I couldn't move, and my knees locked up. I fell to the ground. My thoughts went silent, and Hailey vanished from my mind for a moment.

I completely lost it after that. I started shooting heroin like there was no tomorrow, adding more dope and less water each time. I needed to forget. I had to get her outta my head. Whenever I closed my eyes, all I could picture was her and my so-called friend touching each other. The only time I wasn't thinking about her was when I was high. So I used more and more and more until nothing but using was important, and nothing but addiction remained. I started selling weed around school to keep up with my body's demands for more heroin and more heroin and more heroin.

I lost fifteen pounds in ten days, and my eyes sunk so deep into my skull that I began looking more and more like a skeleton and less like a seventeen-year-old kid. I stopped caring about how I looked, stopped showering as much, slept even less than before, and ate almost nothing. My parents were so worried about me that they sent me to our family doctor to see if maybe I had some kinda disease or something. But I had a few days to prepare for the appointment and spent the night before drinking this awful body-cleansing drink I'd bought on the Internet. It worked, and my urine came up clear—but the doctor told my parents that I should probably go see a shrink, because something seemed really off.

"Again with the psychiatrist? I already went to one of those, remember?"

"Yes, Son," my mom responded. "I do remember—but there's obviously something very wrong with you, and it's the way it has to be. I need someone to tell me what's wrong. I need that."

"Fine. Whatever, but nothing's wrong. I'm just fine. You can send me to all the shrinks you want—it's not gonna change the fact that I'm perfectly okay."

It'd been almost two semesters since my grades had plummeted, and my parents were still in the dark. They'd found out about a few detentions and a few bad grades, but I'd managed to hide away the bulk of them. It was all hanging on by a thread though. I couldn't hold on much longer. I didn't have it in me to keep stashing away report cards, forging stuff, and purposely erasing phone messages. I'd brought my grades up just enough when Hailey and I were still dating to buy a little more time, but they were slipping again. Parent-teacher conferences were coming up at the end of the month, and my parents were dead set on going. It was all falling apart. It was all falling apart so fast.

I still had a couple weeks—a couple weeks to bury myself even further into submission. I was already up to a half a gram of tar a day—about fifty dollars' worth of dope straight into my bloodstream. I had to learn the hard way that I could no longer make it through the school day without using. I was sitting in science class when I became violently ill one afternoon and puked all over myself in front of everyone. I was sweating and shaking and sneezing all at the same time. I ran to the school nurse and told her that the flu was running around in my family, and she let me crash in her office. After that, I started taking a loaded needle with me to inject between classes, or sometimes, I'd take an Afrin nasal spray bottle filled with tar and water to sniff in class. But most of the time, I'd take both.

I started making solo trips downtown around the same time I started pawning off everything I had for money. Desperation drove me to do it. I didn't want Chase and the other guys seeing how down and out I'd gotten, so it seemed only logical that I cut them outta the equation. I was also sick of sharing everything with everyone else. My appetite for heroin was growing more ferocious by the day, and the communal pile of junk wasn't doing it for me anymore. I'd always had this sneaky suspicion that Chase was cutting off a little extra for himself, but I was never able to prove it. It was just a feeling, you know? He was such a smug punk sometimes. He probably thought that since we were always getting high in his basement that he was owed a little extra. I could've easily seen him slicing a tiny piece off for himself and then repackaging the bag as if the dope man had tied it off. Nevertheless, I withdrew myself from the group and started making runs alone.

The first thing I ever pawned for money was my Xbox. I took it to some rundown place in the city, and the guy working there gave me fifty dollars for the thing. I left there feeling grimy all over. That Xbox had once been my prized possession, and there I was selling the thing for fifty measly dollars. I told myself that I'd buy it back before my parents noticed it was missing, but when I finally had the money to get it back, I spent it on extra heroin instead. Actually, I ended up taking the pawn guy more stuff of mine to sell—DVDs, comics, baseball cards, and action figures, to name a few. I chose the stuff carefully, at first. I didn't wanna take anything too big, nothing that my parents would realize was gone until way later. But before I knew it, everything of mine worth anything was gone, so I moved on to selling things that weren't mine, like my father's woodworking tools and my mother's jewelry. I'd stuff as much merchandise as I could into the back of my old Honda and sell it off to the highest bidder. Sometimes, depending on what it was, Shorty would trade outright for the items, but most of the time, I took everything to my pawn guy. He was one of the few who didn't ask questions, but that didn't mean that he was a nice guy. He was making a killing off me. One time I went into his shop and saw a set of video surveillance cameras I'd pawned off to him for a hundred bucks on sale for nine hundred. It made me madder than hell, so I called him out on it.

"I can't believe you only gave me a hundred dollars for that thing. You really think I'm stupid, don't you?"

"No, I think you're a damn junky and a thief. I've been in this business longer than you've been alive. Try and take this crap somewhere else and see how fast they call the cops on you. Don't you ever come to me with that attitude you little preppy punk."

There was so much I wanted to say, but I held back. I needed the old bastard way too much to go screwing things up.

It was right about then that things completely fell apart. It was late one night and I'd gone all day without a single dose of medicine. I was sweating profusely and my hamstrings were throbbing. For whatever reason, withdrawal always hit me in my legs worse than anywhere else.

I didn't have a single dime to spend, but I called Shorty

anyway to see if we could strike a deal of some sort. I was in luck. He told me that his brother was getting outta the penitentiary and needed a set of clothes to help get him through his first couple of days on the outside. He even had a list made up and everything. He read it off to me.

"A Yankees fitted cap, a pair of Nike Air Max '95s, one set of Guess jeans, and a black Polo shirt."

"Damn, man. I dunno if I can grab all that. The mall closes in like an hour and the Air Max's alone are like one fifty. I'll see what I can do though."

"Yeah, see what you can do and I'll meet you at the normal spot."

I hung up the phone and got right to work. I threw on some clothes and asked my mom if she could take me to the mall to grab a new outfit for some made-up event. I don't remember exactly what I told her the stuff was for, but after a few tears and a lotta back and forth, she reluctantly agreed.

I managed to get every last thing on Shorty's list. It was about three hundred dollars in all. I figured I'd get at least a gram for everything, if not a little more. Shorty was usually pretty generous when it came right down to it. But honestly, it wasn't like I had any say in the matter. No matter how little he offered me for the clothes, I was dead set on taking it. The last thing I was gonna do was turn him down and go home empty handed. I'd been down that road before, and I swore up and down that I'd never go back. Dope withdrawals were the worst. They were the absolute worst.

I ran back home before departing downtown to drop off my mom and throw on the outfit I was giving to Shorty. None of it fit, but it was all for show anyway. I just needed an excuse to leave the house that late at night with the car and my new threads.

"I'm gonna go show this stuff off to a few friends and see if they like it, Mom. I'll be right back, okay?"

"It's very late, Son. You have school tomorrow. How long are you going to be?"

"Not long. Like an hour tops."

"I don't know. I don't think it's a very good idea."

"I'm just going down the street, Mom. I'm freaking seventeen years old. What gives?"

"Fine. Just hurry up, Jude. You're only doing this because your father is gone on a business trip. You wouldn't do this if he was home. Just hurry up, please."

I bolted out to the car and was downtown in record time. I went to the meeting spot in an apartment complex off Lucas and Hunt and Highway 70. We'd met there a bunch of times before. I liked the place, because it was right off the highway and only a few minutes from a parking garage that I was partial to shooting up in. It had the perfect amount of light and the perfect number of cars, and there were no security guards in sight. I could do my thing, get right back onto the highway, and be home in thirty minutes flat.

But Shorty was taking his precious time getting to me. I was getting anxious. "What if he leaves me hanging," I thought. "It wouldn't be the first time." I needed to get my fix and hurry home. My gaslight was on, and I hadn't eaten all day. I was shaking all over, but I couldn't tell if it was because I was starving, or because I hadn't shot a single shot since the night before. It had been months since I'd gone that long without dosing, maybe even years.

Shorty finally showed up a good two hours after my arrival in the city. He was evil like that sometimes. I hopped into his car, stripped off the clothes, and handed them over to him. He got a pretty good kick outta the whole thing, like I was some form of amusement for him. In turn, he threw me his entire stash of dope and told me to take what I felt was fair. I was thrown back by his request, but I did it anyway. I broke off a good hundred-dollar piece and left his car wearing a wifebeater and a pair of boxers. That's when it hit me that I hadn't really thought the whole thing through. I had nothing extra to put on, and it was too late to do anything about it. My only hope was that my mom would be asleep when I got back and I'd be able to sneak in unnoticed.

Then my phone rang, and the situation went from bad to worse. It was my mom.

"Jude, I need you home right now. Get home immediately."

She was crying hysterically and could barely speak.

"Mom, what's wrong?"

"Just get home. Please, Son. Now."

The phone clicked, and she hung up. I tried calling back, but nobody answered. There were so many things it could've been. She could've found out about my grades, or she could've discovered something in my room, or she could've noticed how much was missing around the house or found a pawn receipt or a needle—the possibilities were endless. I was getting sloppy, and my brain wasn't working like it used to. I could've easily left something lying out. *Dammit.* She'd be waiting for me the moment I walked in, and she'd see that I wasn't wearing the outfit she'd gotten me. Suddenly, my breathing got really heavy and I got this pain in my stomach like you wouldn't believe.

I pulled away from where I'd met Shorty and drove a block down the street to the parking garage I was set to shoot up in. I needed a shot to calm my nerves. I turned the heat on full blast to raise my veins and parked in a spot between two dusty cars. I began cooking up immediately. I unwrapped the plastic wrap around the H and cut a chunk in half with my fingers. I put it in the spoon and threw a capful of water on top. I was in a rush, but I slowed down just enough to make sure nothing got messed up. When I was done cooking, I slurped the stuff into my syringe, licked the tip of the needle clean, and flicked the thing to get all the air bubbles out.

I sat there and stuck myself for ten minutes before getting the poison into my bloodstream. It was taking longer and longer each time to hit a vein. There was scar tissue, and there were scabs and bruises, and my arms were swollen in some places. I pushed every bit of the liquid in. Halfway through, though, the needle pulled out of my vein, and the dope slipped under my skin. It burned like acid, and my arm swelled up instantaneously. It itched and it burned. It hurt tremendously. Worse than the pain was that I'd missed half the shot, but the half that did get through was just enough to wash away most of the sickness. I stopped sweating. I stopped shaking. My breathing returned back to normal. I lit a cigarette and pulled outta the lot slowly. My gaslight beeped the entire way home, and my arm swelled up like a sausage. I was shirtless, bottomless, shoeless, starving, and my arm looked like a rattlesnake had bitten it—but at least I wasn't sick anymore.

My car died the second I pulled into the garage at home. My mom was waiting for me. As I walked into the house, her face became expressionless. She took one look at my arms and hit the floor like a ton of bricks. I'd been in such a daze that I'd forgotten to wipe the blood off my arms after shooting up.

"What have you done to yourself, Son?" she screamed. "What have you done?"

Finally realizing the problem, I took off upstairs to my room, threw on a long-sleeved shirt and a pair of shorts, and ran back down to fix things with my mother. She was in hysterics—crying and rambling on incoherently. I dug deep within myself to find the words to say something, anything, that would make her better, but I couldn't think of a single thing. I couldn't even bring myself to cry, or feel bad. I was emotionless. My poor mother was lying on the floor in the fetal position crying because of me, and I couldn't conjure up a single freaking emotion—not even one. I moved close to her to help her up, and that's when I saw all the stuff in the corner of the room. It was all there—my needles and pot scales and sandwich bags and spoons and pawn receipts and report cards. Everything. She'd found it all.

My first thought was to run. My next thought was to lie through my teeth about everything and then shoot up afterwards and forget about what'd happened. As I got closer, my mom's words became clearer and clearer. She just kept saying "why" over and over and over again. I took a seat on the couch, put my head in my hands, and nodded off.

Twenty minutes went by before we exchanged words.

"Jude. What is this stuff? What is this? I don't understand what's happening. Why do your arms look like that? What happened to your clothes? Tell me, Son. What's happening?"

I opened my eyes and sat up straight.

"Mom, it's not what you think—"

"It's not what I think? Look at your arms. Look at all this stuff on the table. It all makes sense now. I thought I was going crazy, but it all makes sense."

"Mom—"

"*No,*" she cried out angrily. "*Don't 'Mom' me.* You've been lying to us this whole time. How could you? How long? How long have you been doing it?"

"Mom, please."

"*How long?*"

"I dunno—a little over a year, I guess."

"A year? You've been doing this a year? How? How?"

"I'm not gonna tell you that. It just happened, okay. It just did, and then some other stuff happened, and I started doing a little more, but I'm fine now. I know how bad this looks, but I'm not addicted or anything. I can stop whenever."

"Enough. I've heard enough. You're sick, Son. Don't you get that? You're sick. I don't even know how to tell your father about this. He's going to be home any minute with your sister, so I suggest you go to your room and get yourself together. Your father will know what to do."

"This is bullshit, Mom. I'm fine, dammit. I'm okay. I don't need to *do* anything. You just go in my room, and take all my stuff out. How could you?"

"Excuse me? How could *I?* How could *I?* It's my house, and I'm not the one naked with blood running down my arm and a hundred needles in my room. Am I? Don't you dare turn this around on me."

"Whatever—go to hell, Mom. I hate you. You're dead to me."

I don't know where the words came from, but they did,

and there was no taking them back. It was the worst thing I'd ever said to her. Her face became gray and hopeless. I ran upstairs to my room and tucked myself under the covers in my bed. I was furious. I was furious that I'd been so reckless and furious that my mom had taken all my stuff and furious that things would never be the same again. My secret was out. My parents would be forever suspicious of me from that day forward. I would no longer be able to get away with anything at all. They'd watch my every move and probably take away my car and never give me money again and listen to me through the walls and on the phones. My run had come to an end.

My dad came home a while later, and twenty minutes after that, screaming ensued. I imagined my mom had told him about everything, and they were fighting about what to do with me or who was to blame or whatever. A single tear rolled down my cheek and hit me in the hand. It'd been a long time since I last cried. I didn't understand what was making me so upset. My emotions were all tied up in knots. Another tear hit my hand and then a bunch of them. I decided to do a small shot to kill whatever it was that was making me sad. I locked the door, cooked up, dosed a bit, and then rocked back and forth on my bed. I stared blankly at the wall in front of me and rocked—back and forth, back and forth, back and forth. My tears stopped, and I fell asleep.

CHAPTER 6

THE PROGRAM

Almost two years after I first tried heroin, I was off to rehab for the first time. I didn't really have a choice in the matter. The day after my mom had discovered my cache of paraphernalia, her and my dad pulled me outta school and threatened to kick me outta the house if I didn't go. I figured the only way to get them off my back was to go along with their plan to fix me, although I had no intention of getting better. I mean, my life was in shambles, and I was going nowhere fast, but I wasn't convinced that I needed help. I was sure that I could taper down and do away with my habit on my own, if, and when, the time was right. It just wasn't then. I wasn't ready to stop. My bed stand shots were the only thing I looked forward to and the only thing that kept me going. How was I supposed to live a life where I didn't wake up and spike my vein first thing in the morning? It'd become my sole purpose for existing.

The place was called Horizon. It was a hospital-based inpatient and outpatient facility serving both adults and adolescents with issues ranging from anorexia to substance abuse. It was one of the most highly recommended rehabs in the state of Missouri, and also one of the most expensive—something like thirty grand for a sixty-day stay. They cut my father a small financial break given his occupation and given how he'd sent a good deal of his own clients to Horizon for help with their own drug demons. To tell you the truth, I think they just felt altogether bad for him more than anything. I mean, dropping me off at rehab had to have been one of the worst experiences of his life. I'd never seen the man more lost and scared.

The morning I left for rehab, I mainlined an enormous shot of dope and snuck a joint in the shower. I rolled up a few more, stuck them in my sock for safekeeping, and dripped Visine into my bloodshot eyes. It was the last of my pot, and almost the last of my junk. I figured I'd have enough to get me through the next day, but after that, I'd either hafta make something happen, or risk getting sick. And I sure as hell wasn't prepared to get sick. The thought alone terrified me.

Before I emerged from the bathroom, I looked at myself in the mirror for the first time in weeks. I looked like a different person altogether. My skin was bloated in some places and sunken in others. My eyes were empty, dark, and non-responsive. I'd lost so much weight too. I barely recognized myself.

"Let's go!" my father screamed at me from the bottom of the stairs. "*Now.*"

"I'm comin' dammit," I shot back. "Just gimme a second."

It was time. I threw my needle and dope into an air vent, took a deep breath, and hustled out to the car.

My relationship with my parents had reached an all-time low. They were trying to ruin what I had with heroin, and for that reason—they'd become my nemeses. The three of us hadn't had a normal conversation in months, and whenever we did exchange words, it was because I'd done something wrong. I can't tell you how many times my father and I'd gotten into it about my erratic behavior. I think the thing that made him more upset than anything was that he couldn't figure out what was wrong with me. It wasn't until my mom found all that stuff in my room that it finally dawned on him that I was on drugs.

A lotta people ask me why my father wasn't able to put it together sooner, with him being a drug counselor and all. The simple fact is that he just couldn't. I was sneaky, and he was busy as hell, and maybe a tiny bit in denial. Even if my parents had recognized the signs and gotten tough sooner, I don't know if it would've done any good. Aside from my parents chaining me to a bedrail, I don't see what they could've done to make it all better. I would've kept sneaking out at night, kept pawning my valuables for money, and kept using.

We drove for forty minutes in complete silence to the rehab center. I sat in the backseat planning the next dope run in my head the entire time. I had to devise a scheme to get downtown without a car or any money, and with my parents glued to my side. It was an impossible situation, but my will to avoid sickness was at an all-time high. It was all I could think about. If I didn't come up with a plan fast, I was convinced that I'd end up dying from heroin withdrawal. Of course, I'd never gone without heroin long enough to experience full-out withdrawal, but that didn't stop me from being deathly afraid of it.

Two annoyingly chipper counselors, a man and a woman with ear-to-ear smiles and extended hands, greeted us at the door as we pulled up to the sprawling facility. They introduced themselves as Sabrina Davis and Dr. Ben Scott.

"We're all so glad to have you here, Jude," the lady, Mrs. Davis, opened up with. "First, and foremost, how about I get you settled into your room while Dr. Scott here has a quick chat with your parents?"

"Yeah, sure. I guess that's okay," I responded, annoyed.

I looked at my parents one last time and nodded goodbye. They just stared past me for a second and then quickly turned back toward the doctor. I'd never seen them look so lifeless and unhappy. My father was usually a bit sterner than others, but my mother, well, it probably took everything in her to look so distraught. She was usually so good about putting on a happy face in the face of adversity, but looking at her right then you would've never believed she'd smiled a single day in her life.

I followed Mrs. Davis up the walkway and through a set of double glass doors into the main waiting area. We walked past a reception desk and through a carpeted hallway to a separate wing on the left side of the building. The place smelled like Lysol and medical supplies and looked just as I'd imagined it would, like a hospital. The walls on both sides of the fluorescent-lit hallway were covered with patient artwork, inspirational quotes, and staff photos from what looked like weekend getaways. I walked closely behind Mrs. Davis. She was decently pretty for a middle-aged lady. She had a slim body with a tight butt and a pretty face. Her hair was blonde, except for a few dark accents scattered throughout, and her skin was brilliantly clear, except for a birthmark that ran down the top part of her shoulder.

We stopped at a room about halfway down the hall and walked in. It was decent looking for what it was worth—blueberry-colored walls, linoleum floors, a leather couch, a crappy desk, an old rocking chair, and a lamp.

"Your counselor, Mike, should be here any minute to walk you through orientation," Mrs. Davis announced. "Is there anything I can bring you? Water, a snack—anything?"

"No—I'm alright, but thanks."

"Okay, well if you need anything, just let me know. I'll be right around the corner in my office."

"Alright, will do. Where is everyone, by the way?"

"Well, most of the patients are in group. You don't have to worry about that today though. All you'll be doing is orientation stuff, and tomorrow, you'll most likely start going to groups."

I nodded, and Mrs. Davis smiled before walking off. I was alone, finally. My high was beginning to fade, and I was getting anxious. I wanted to smoke a joint, but I figured it probably wasn't the best idea considering I'd only been there exactly five minutes. So, I held off and paced the room instead.

On the table beside the couch was a pile of newspapers that someone had left behind. I picked up the top paper and looked it over. It'd been months since I'd read a newspaper or flipped through a magazine, or even watched a full movie without passing out before the end. I was completely outta touch with the world outside of my own, except for the stuff we talked about in school. 9/11 had just happened, the country was on the brink of war, the economy was on the brink of collapse, and all I could think about was how I was gonna make my junk quota for the day. It wasn't that I didn't care; I just didn't have the time or energy to pay attention to anything but the daily grind.   All I could think about was getting home to my stash, and how good it was gonna feel to have a needle under my skin, and what my next move was gonna be. I can't say that I enjoyed getting high anymore—it'd become a full-time job to keep up with my body's demands for more and more dope. It was a chase that never stopped. I was always either in the act of getting high or in the act of getting the stuff to get high with—buying needles, and scraping up money, and driving downtown, and finding collapsed veins to shoot up in. I didn't even know what it meant to be normal anymore either. The whole concept seemed so far from being possible. Normal to me was being high. It was the only time I had the energy to do anything. When I wasn't high, I was completely devoid of all life.

A good twenty minutes went by before a man with a red ponytail came to my door. He was short, skinny, and gentle looking. He had a whiskery-looking mustache that covered up the top part of his mouth, and his eyebrows did the same with the tops of his eyes. He squinted when he smiled and made this funny-sounding wheezing noise in between breaths.

"Jude?"

"Yeah?"

"Jude, I'm Mike, your counselor. You mind if I come in?"

"No, not at all."

"I'll make it quick. I just wanted to introduce myself and get a few signatures from you. Ten minutes, tops."

"Yeah, okay."

"Okay, great. First off, do you have a cell phone or any contraband, like drugs or paraphernalia?"

"No. My parents took my cell from me, and I wouldn't dare bring drugs into the place. What am I? Crazy?"

"No, no—just had to ask. We work off the honor system here. That means we're not gonna go rummaging through your stuff, but if we suspect anything, we reserve the right to do that."

"Fair enough."

"Okay, let's get started, then."

We shook hands and sat down beside one another on the couch. He scooted to within an inch of me and looked me over for a few. His breath reeked of coffee and cigarettes. I stared at the ground and subtly covered my nose to fight off the smell.

"You're not lookin' too hot, bud. Heroin, right?"

"I guess. I mean, that's what my parents have me in here for."

"And how old are you?"

"Seventeen."

"Wow. Seventeen, huh? You guys are getting younger and younger every year, it seems like. Look, in all seriousness, though, I'm no stranger to heroin. I shot the stuff for twenty years, and lost everything because of it—my wife, kids, job, home, savings—everything. You remind me a lot of myself when I was just starting out. I know you can't see it now, but we're all just here to help. This is all for you, Jude."

"Yeah, well, I kinda think it's a waste. I'm willing to listen to what you all hafta say, but I just don't think I need all this. I can quit if I want."

"Then why haven't you?"

"Because I've only done it a few times, and I don't see the big deal."

"Okay, fair enough, but that's not what your parents are saying, and I'm sure if you pulled up your sleeves right now, your arms would tell a completely different story. But we won't get into all that right now. I came here for your signature, so, one thing at a time."

"Fine, whatever."

He took a deep breath to clear the red outta his face and handed me a pen to sign with. I could tell I was getting to him. I wasn't trying to be rude or anything—I just didn't like talking to guys about my feelings. I would've been better off with someone like Mrs. Davis. I don't know why, but it was a lot simpler for me to confide in women. I guess it was just a motherly thing—like, I'd always felt comfortable telling my mom stuff, but not my dad.

I buried my head into my hands and tried my best to fade away. He cleared his throat and started up again.

"We work off the twelve steps here at Horizon. You're enrolled in the outpatient program, which means you'll be here from nine-to-five every day, and then you go home at night. What that doesn't mean is that you screw around after you leave. We'll know if you are; trust me. Just try and keep up with your nightly meetings, readings, and assignments—and you'll be just fine. Okay?"

I quickly raised my head up outta my sweaty palms,

thought, and rethought about what he'd said about nightly meetings. Mike looked at me and squinted his eyes suspiciously. Everything about the guy screamed "junky"— from his dumbfounded looks to his glassy eyes and rugged appearance. That's the thing about addicts—we can recognize one another from across the room. Even if he hadn't told me he shot dope for twenty years, I would've known. Of course, I didn't consider myself to be an addict at the time, but that didn't mean I wasn't one. I just hadn't figured it out yet.

"What was that last part about nightly meetings?" I finally asked.

"Well, you're expected to attend one meeting, NA or AA, each evening after you leave. They're just as important as the day-to-day stuff. You need to find a sponsor, too, someone that'll sign off on your attendance sheet as you go. Your sponsor needs to be someone trustworthy, preferably someone who's been a sponsor before and has experience with it. You want to find the right person, and until you do, just have whoever's conducting the meetings sign off on your sheets. Does that answer your question?"

"Yeah, I got it. I just didn't hear what you said. I got it now though. Thanks."

I did my best to hold in my enthusiasm, but I was bursting at the seams. I'd figured it out—the plan. I'd figured out a way to get downtown without anybody knowing: I'd use the nightly meetings to get everything I needed to score: a car, some money, and a two-hour window. I knew the moment the words rolled off his tongue that it was right. Even if it worked only once or twice, that'd be one or two less times I'd hafta worry about being sick. It was perfect. Immediate relief set in.

"Our rules are pretty straightforward," Mike continued. "Don't test positive for drugs, don't be disruptive in group, respect others, and don't ever, ever bring contraband into the facility. If you understand these rules, sign here on the line."

He handed me a clipboard, and I signed the paper and handed it back to him. I was starting to feel really nasty all over—shivers and sweats, to start with. I could feel the dope leaving my body. It was a brutal and unforgiving feeling. I tried to stay positive and think about getting home. I tried so hard to focus on something other than how crappy I felt, but every time I got my mind off the stuff, it came back just as fast. Mostly, I wanted Mike to leave me the hell alone. The guy wouldn't shut up.

"We're pretty unorthodox here at Horizon. We believe that patients can help each other more than other facilities are willing to allow. Our strength as a group comes from the inspiration of a Higher Power."

He handed me a plain-looking blue book with the words "Alcoholics Anonymous" printed across the top.

"It's all in this book here. You need to read that as often as you can—between groups, at home, in the car—whenever. I know you're doing makeup work for school right now, but just try and find some time to familiarize yourself with it. The truth is in there, brother. It's all in that book."

"Okay, I'll take a look at it."

"Right on. Well, I'm gonna head out, but let me just finish up by saying that this is a voluntary program, and the front door is always open. This program is highly successful if you put forth the effort and work the steps. It works if you work it, and it doesn't if you don't. That's something you'll hear over and over again—it works if you work it."

He looked at me one last time.

"Okay, well, Dr. Scott will be in to see you shortly."

He shook my hand and left the room. I was alone again. I tilted my head back against the wall behind the couch and held my eyes closed tight. My head was pounding, my legs were beginning to cramp up, and my stomach was racing around like a waterslide. I kept my eyes closed and thought about my score. I plotted out exactly what I was gonna say to my parents, what they'd say back, and what I'd say in return. I plotted out a backup plan in case Plan A fell through—I'd hafta steal something, something big. Credit cards were always good—a hundred dollars of gas in the dope man's car was worthy of at least a thirty-piece of junk, or I could just take him shopping at the mall and hope that the clerk didn't check the name on the card. They hardly ever did.

It wasn't gonna be easy though. Right before my parents checked me into Horizon, they'd gathered up everything of value from around the house and locked it all up in a safe at the bank. They'd also begun sleeping with their pocketbooks and writing their names and phone number on every TV and computer in the house in permanent marker, which made the stuff damn near impossible to pawn. Pawning was getting tiring anyway.

I was almost asleep when I heard someone call out my name. I looked up, saw who it was, and put my head back down. It was Dr. Scott—the goofy-looking doctor I'd met outside when my parents and I pulled up. The guy must've been like seven feet tall. He had a bulging belly and was bald on top but made up for it on his face and body. He wore designer glasses, a pocket protector, mismatched socks, and a stained doctor's coat and stank of Stetson cologne.

"I know today's probably already been a hectic day for you, but I need to get some more info about you before I can prescribe anything."

"Prescribe?" I mumbled with my eyes still closed.

"Well, yeah—just in case you need medication to help out while you're here. Mostly, though, I just wanna get a little background history from you. I need you to fill out this form. Actually, it's a couple of forms, more like questionnaires, but they're pretty self-explanatory. It'll help give me a better understanding of what we need to do to help you. Now, you're going to want to answer them as honestly as possible, okay?"

He slid the two questionnaires across the table, and I started on the first one. I answered them honestly.

Do you feel anxious? YES.

Are you sad or depressed? YES.

Are you suicidal? NO.

Do you resent being given advice? YES.

Are people trustworthy? NO.

Are you uncomfortable around others? YES.

There were about twenty questions in all. I finished the form, handed it back to him, and began the next one—The Mood Disorder Questionnaire.

Do you have more energy than normal? YES.

Do you have trouble with spending money? YES.

Do you think about sex more than usual? YES.

Do you speak faster than normal at times? YES.

Do you experience highs and lows? YES.

Again, I answered them honestly, perhaps a bit too honestly. I handed the last form back to the doctor, and he quietly looked over them.

"Now, I think it's safe to say that you're experiencing a lot of changes in your life, Jude," the doctor started. "What we're worried about here is that you are stunting your growth and development by using all these mind-altering substances at such a critical age. Based on the answers you've provided here, it's apparent to me that you're manically depressed."

I sighed, took in a deep breath, and smiled arrogantly.

"We see this kind of thing all the time," he continued. "You probably feel like the only time you're happy is when you're high, right? Well, there's a name for what you're doing— it's called self-medication. You're stabilizing your moods with drugs, but all you're really doing is pushing yourself further into a hole. Let me ask you this: Have you ever been on medication before? Did your previous therapist recommend anything? Or, how about history—is there any history of depression, or abuse, in your family?"

I took a second before answering.

"No. The shrink I went to didn't say anything about being depressed, and I dunno about history or anything. Nobody in my family has ever done drugs, and nothing bad has ever happened to me—if that's what you mean. I just got high a few times and liked it. I mean, everyone at school either drinks or gets high, somehow. Are they all depressed?"

"No—you're not hearing me. Some people make bad choices, yes—but with you, it's different. You're getting high because you have a chemical imbalance, not because you're curious or are having a good time, necessarily. It might've started that way, but let's be honest—are you still enjoying yourself?"

I wouldn't have said it in a million years, but the bastard was right. The "getting high" routine had gotten old, and the only reason I still did get high was to feel better. Even with pot—I'd smoke the stuff, and once the high faded, I was miserable again.

"Let's do this," he broke in. "Let's get you on a light anti-depressant, and we'll see where it goes. Okay?"

"What about my sickness? Are you gonna give me something for that?"

"By sickness, I assume you're referring to withdrawals?"

"No, never mind. I just meant the aches and stuff."

"Jude, I know it's hard to admit that you're an addict, but it's the first step in our twelve-step process. You have to hear yourself say the words, 'I'm an addict.' It's the same with meds. If you can't just come out and admit that you're in withdrawal and need help, then you're not gonna make it very far. That's the cold, hard truth."

"Well, I'm not."

"Well, Jude, your body says different. Your mind says different. Your pride is getting in the way of you getting better. You're too young and smart to do that. Now, let's get your blood pressure and a urine sample before I write a prescription for anything, okay? We'll send you home with some meds to help ease the pain a little bit. Don't worry."

I got up and followed him out to the nurse's station. My whole body felt like it was gonna crumble. I'd perspired so much in the past hour that I'd soaked through my boxers and undershirt. I couldn't stop yawning either. I would've done anything to get something in me to make me feel better. If my parents hadn't dropped me off, and my car wasn't at the house, it would've been damn hard not to leave, probably impossible. The last thing I was thinking about was getting clean.

It was two o'clock, and groups were beginning to let out throughout the building. It was the first time I'd seen anyone besides staff. It was like watching a herd of sheep split off into two—one half went outside to smoke and the other to the nurse's station to med-up. Dr. Humphrey introduced to me to a nurse named Sally, and almost immediately, she started singing "Hey Jude." She stopped after the opening chorus and then, outta nowhere, pointed to my right arm.

"Can you lift up your sleeve, please?"

I maybe thought she was looking for track marks, which I had a lot of, but she pulled out a blood pressure kit instead. I smiled. My right arm wasn't as bad as my left, because I'm right-handed and favored shooting with my right, but that only meant that my left arm was ten times worse off. There was one spot that was worse than anywhere else—right where my left bicep and forearm met. There was a small abscess that was starting to form right around there, and the veins up and down my arm were all burnt up, but I still shot up in the damn thing because it's where I had the most success. I kept thinking the veins would come back, but they were gone—tucked under scar tissue and needle marks.

I pulled up my sleeve and hung my arm out in front of the nurse. She wrapped the blood pressure band around my arm, pumped it tight, and then released.

Once she was done with that, she handed me a cup to pee in and asked Dr. Scott if he'd accompany me. He said yes, and the two of us walked to a small room off to the side of the nurse's station. I say "room," because it wasn't a complete bathroom—there was no sink or soap or paper towels, only a lone toilet bowl with blue water. I'm guessing it was to keep people from messing with their urine samples.

I was starting to feel more light-headed than before, but I had to keep going. I had to keep going, so I could make it to the nightly meeting and get my fix. I had to keep going and show my parents that I was enthusiastic about getting better so they'd be more inclined to give me what I needed, money and all that. I could've easily given up, and given in to the sickness, and fallen down on all fours; that's how crappy I felt. But I couldn't. I couldn't. I had to keep going. I knew once I got that syringe steady in my vein and released the poison inside, everything would go back to normal, and all the day's hardships would be forgotten. Until then, though, I had to keep going.

The doctor stood right beside me as I held the cup right up to my front side and did my best to piss. Nothing. It was impossible to go with another man looking down at me when I was most exposed.

"Just think of waterfalls," he said, smirking.

I wanted to kill him. I was growing sicker, less tolerant, and more irrational by the second. I probably would've killed him if I could've gotten away with it. I closed my eyes and tried to think of a happy place, and after a minute or so, I filled the cup up halfway.

"Perfect. Now let's get you some Gatorade and a couple ibuprofens to help with the withdrawals. I'm going to prescribe a mild sedative to help you sleep at night, but I want you to take ibuprofen every five hours for the pain. If things get really bad, we can give you clonidine, but that's about as far as we'll go here with the hard stuff. I'm also going to prescribe that anti-depressant I was telling you about. It takes a couple weeks before you actually feel the effects, but I'm thinking it's going to really help calm things down for you a bit."

I couldn't believe what I was hearing. *Ibuprofen?* Maybe I'd just become way too dependent on drugs, but ibuprofen wasn't gonna do a damn thing to help me along. The stuff barely worked when I had a headache. I might as well have taken nothing at all. I needed opiates—opiates were the only thing that would make me feel better. That's what I'd been conditioned to believe anyway. I was blind to anything else. I headed to my room wincing in pain.

I was lying on my couch imagining the possibility of being at Horizon for another month, when a young girl with curly black hair entered my room. She had intensely green eyes with long eyelashes and wore blue eye shadow, light pink lip-gloss, and heavy bronzer. There were thick bandages wrapped around each of her wrists.

"Hey," she said softly. "I'm Tyra. You're Jude, right?"

"Yeah, I'm Jude. Do I know you?"

"No, but the girl I'm rooming with does. I guess you guys go to school together or something. She saw you in the hallway and told me who you were, and I just wanted to come by and say hey. It's good to have another young person here. I'm only fifteen, and everyone else is like my parents' age. I can't stand this place."

"It's that bad, huh?"

"Yeah, well, they all look at me like I'm a freaking sick puppy or something, and I can't stand it. They stare at my bandages all day and look at me with pity in their eyes, and I don't need their damn pity. I'm fine."

"Yeah, I hear you. What happened, if you don't mind me asking?"

"I tried to kill myself. I sliced my wrists and took a bunch of pills, but they brought me back to life. They said my heart stopped, and I was dead for a bit, and then I was alive."

I was thrown back by her candor.

"Why? I mean, why did you do it?"

"Because my parents threatened to send me here. I'm not even addicted to drugs. I've done ecstasy a few times and drink just like everyone else, but it doesn't affect me. I make a perfect G.P.A in school, and am headed to Vanderbilt, for God's sake. The only reason I'm here is because my mom found a note in my room that some guy sent to me about getting high after school. She said she was gonna send me to rehab, and that's when I did it—with my dad's straight razor. Now, they have me on so much medication that I can barely keep my head up. I have no personality anymore. I'm like a robot."

"I know exactly how you feel—my parents are the same way," I spoke openly. "They expect so much outta me. And I know what you mean about the medicine thing too—the doctor diagnosed me with manic depression in like five minutes. I thought I was in here to get off drugs, not take more."

"Ha, are you serious?" she laughed. "He diagnosed me with the same thing. Did he give you the test?"

"Yeah, the two-part questionnaire?"

"Yup, exactly. This place is so full of shit. They diagnose you in five minutes and then move on to the next person. We're like test subjects to them."

It felt good to talk. She sat down beside me on the couch, and we talked like we'd known each other for years. Her story was tragic, and her thoughts about the future were even darker. She had no hope that she would ever get better.

"It's always about money; that's all my parents care about," she said. "It's all about medical school and SATs and soccer and dance. I can't remember the last time I did something for myself. I can't even remember the last time I laughed or smiled or the last time my parents told me they loved me. What if I don't want to be a doctor like my dad or a lawyer like my mom? I can't tell them that. I just can't. They wouldn't understand."

Listening to Tyra and her misery kinda made me feel hopeful about my own life. I know that's a horrible thing to say, but it's just one of those things that you can't control. I mean, I just couldn't imagine wanting to kill myself. Her pain must've been so immense that she felt like suicide was her only way out. Maybe she was just crying out, but still, that just seemed like an awfully risky way to cry out. Things were getting pretty dark in my world, but the thought of killing myself had never once crossed my mind.

The two of us talked until it was time to go home, said goodbye, and walked out of the room together. My mother was waiting for me on a bench in the waiting room. Our eyes connected. She walked over to me, gave me a hug, and looked into my eyes as if she were staring into my soul.

"How's it going, Son?"

"Not too bad, Mom. I'm doing a lot better, actually."

We walked outside, and she gently grabbed me by the arm. It hurt like hell. My whole body was throbbing.

"The doctor tells me you're not feeling too well?"

"Yeah, I think I was just dehydrated or something. I'm okay though."

But I wasn't okay. I was on the verge of puking, and my nose wouldn't stop running, and I felt like dying. My body was screaming for relief, but I had to keep composed. If she sensed that I wasn't feeling all that great or wasn't all that excited about rehab, my whole plan would've gone to hell. I had to somehow make her think that the whole nightly meeting thing was her idea; then, and only then, would she feel comfortable enough to give me money and a car. If it didn't work out exactly as I'd imagined it, I'd hafta resort to doing something else outta desperation. I closed my eyes and cleared my throat.

"So they have this meeting tonight that I'm supposed to go to. They're like an hour and a half long, but I dunno. What do you think?"

"Tonight?"

"Yeah, tonight. I hafta get a sponsor and stuff."

"Well, I can drive you, and we can get dinner together. But no matter what, if they say you have to go, then you have to go."

"Yeah, I know, but I kinda hafta go alone. The doctor says it's important that I take the initiative to get better by myself. I'll just drop you off at the house and get it over with, okay? I have a prescription I hafta pick up too. I don't know if I have enough for dinner and medicine."

"They didn't feed you?"

"No, I wasn't feeling all that great, but I'm starving now."

"Okay, I'll give you a few dollars, but don't be late coming home. Your father doesn't want you out alone at all, but since this is part of the program—I'm sure he'll understand."

"Okay, I'll just go to the meeting, grab my prescription from the pharmacy, and come home."

"Prescriptions? How much are those gonna be?"

"I'm not sure, probably around fifty or so."

"Okay."

I'd stooped to an all-time low, using my position as a rehab patient to get high. I was in disbelief that it'd worked, and that it'd come together so effortlessly. There was once a time when my mom could look into my eyes and read me like a book, but those times were long gone. There was nothing left to read. I was hollow inside.

CHAPTER 7

HITTING BOTTOM

Three days. Three freaking days—that's how long it took before I was tossed outta rehab for using. Actually, I used the entire time I was at Horizon, but it took them three days to catch me in the act. I was sitting in group in my usual spot next to Tyra listening to the usual addict tirades when they came for me. I'd just finished sticking myself in the bathroom, and the initial rush was still ringing in my ears. I was recklessly high.

I knew the moment I saw them standing there that my run had come to an end. I looked at Tyra and grabbed her hand as if to say goodbye. I knew that I'd most likely never see her again, and the two of us had grown to be as thick as thieves since we'd first met. We ate together, and passed notes to one another, and even held hands when no one was looking. But it wasn't a sexual thing. It was just that we had a lot in common and we were at Horizon for all the same reasons—to satisfy our parents and because we had no other choice. I'm sure we came off as a couple of snooty little brats to the old-timers who were there to legitimately get clean, and I say that because one of them told me just that. Her name was Desiree. She was a crack addict who'd spent her entire life in and outta rehabs and jails, and had lost everything there was to lose because of her addiction. She said that it was "only a matter of time before one of us bottomed out and realized that we blew an opportunity to get better before it got worse." I swear that lady put some kinda curse on me, because right after she said that, really bad things started happening.

They came into the room all at once—Mrs. Davis, Dr. Scott, Nurse Sally, and two other random people. One of them got up right behind me and whispered into my ear. I think it was Mrs. Davis.

"Hey, Jude. Can we see you for a moment in the hall?"

I don't know why they needed five people to escort me out, but I simply got up, smiled at Tyra—and walked out. The charade was over. I was sure of it. The only thing I didn't know was why. I'd broken just about every rule in the place, and every one of them was reason enough to kick me out. As if things weren't already bad enough, I remembered that I had a quarter gram of junk in my sock, a tightly rolled joint in my shirt pocket, and a bag of dirty needles tucked away under the couch in my room. I had enough crap on me to get me locked up for a good year if it got right down to it. I started to panic. Oddly enough though, the only thing I was worried about was losing my stuff.

We walked for what seemed like forever to a barely lit part of the building and entered a room at the end of a blank corridor. I was disoriented by the time we got there. My parents were already waiting in the room when I walked in. My dad's eyes were damn near bulging outta his head, and my mom looked like she'd been crying for days. My bag of dirty needles was sitting on a desk in the middle of the room with a pile of discharge papers neatly stacked under it. Suddenly, my chest tightened up, and I could barely breathe. I'm quite sure I was having a panic attack. I had to get outta there.

Someone asked me to sit down, and all I remember is everything turning red. I completely flipped out.

"No, you can all go to hell. You gave me *ibuprofen*—what'd you expect me to do? I don't need your stupid program anyway. I can stop using if I want, and whenever I want. I don't need any of this. I'm gone."

I grabbed my needles off the desk and stormed out in a rage. I could hear my mom call my name.

"Jude, Jude—please, Son. Come back."

But there was no chance in hell that I was going back. I rushed outta the place and ran outta the first exit door I could find. I must've run ten blocks before slowing down. I found a half-smoked cigarette on the ground and lit it to calm my nerves. I jumped into a phone booth at the corner of two intersecting streets and dialed the only friend whose number I had memorized—Chase. I hadn't seen the kid since I'd been in rehab, but we'd gone our separate ways way before then—everyone in the original crew had. Markus was locked up in some city jail with a fifty thousand-dollar bond for forging a bunch of checks and cleaning out his sister's jewelry box, and Tommy and Davey had been sent off to live with their uncle in Wyoming after their mom found a bunch of weed and H in their dresser drawer.

Chase came and picked me up from the side of the road within an hour, and we were in the city not even twenty minutes after that. I was feeling pretty guilty for leaving my parents at the hospital like that, and couldn't get my mom's last facial expression outta my head. She'd looked absolutely devastated, like her will to live had been ripped outta her. Even after I spiked my vein with enough junk to kill most people, her face was still there. I couldn't get rid of it. It was burned into my consciousness forever.

I didn't go home for a full month after that day. I stayed with Chase at his parents' house and forgot about school and prom and graduation—not like I was gonna graduate anyway. My mom and dad were so pissed off at me that they didn't really seem to mind my absence. They'd switched roles from being my parents to being protectors of their home, and everything in it, including my sister. I kinda liked not having anyone to answer to but the dopeman, and my insatiable appetite for junk, though. Actually, the list had grown to three dopemen since Shorty. You see—everyone from the suburbs mostly went to the same group of guys to get H. Whenever a kid overdosed on a bad batch, the dealer responsible for selling them the stuff—whether it was Shorty or Lil' D or Mario—would crawl underground until the cops disappeared and people stopped asking questions. They'd come outta hiding with a new everything—phone, car, haircut, and home—and deny, deny, deny that they were the ones responsible.

I learned my lesson the hard way when Shorty went underground after a sixteen-year-old suburban girl OD'd on a batch of China White heroin he'd laced with fentanyl to make it more potent. They found the poor girl sitting in her car in an Applebee's parking lot with a needle still in her arm. She'd been dead for over ten hours. Nobody saw or heard from him for three straight months, and I was left high and dry until Markus hooked me up with two new suppliers. Their stuff was decent, but they were hardly ever on time, and half the time, they never showed up at all. I was just another dope fiend to them, after all.

Chase and I began ripping people off like there was no tomorrow. Cokeheads were probably the easiest to get over on. It was a quick way to get money, and it wasn't hard to do by any means. We'd just put a bunch of baking soda in a bag and hustle it off at parties to unsuspecting freshman and sophomores, basically anyone we weren't friends with. We made a lotta enemies doing it, and on a few occasions, people came after us wanting their money back. It got so bad that we had to hide out for a while, because there were so many people wanting to beat the snot outta us for getting over on them. Their money was long gone though—gone the moment we got our hands on it.

The other way we sustained our habits was by using the old receipt trick Markus had told us about long before. We'd try and hit as many stores as we could in any given night and then use every last penny on H. If we were lucky, we'd walk away with a couple hundred dollars a night. But then the stores started catching on to our return scam, and we had to back off for a while. It was a major blow to our pockets, but there was always some other scam to line our pockets down the line. Like, forging checks or just flat-out stealing. It didn't hurt that we looked decent on the outside and seemed completely normal to most people. You never would've guessed that we were junkies—sick maybe—but not junkies. Not in a million years. Nobody ever saw us coming.

On one particular night about a week after I was kicked outta Horizon, Chase and I were pulled over in the city for suspicious activity, and by that, I mean we were pulled for looking suspicious, not doing anything suspicious. We were exiting a McDonald's drive-through when they flagged us down. There was so much crap laying around the inside of the car that it wasn't even worth trying to hide—soda can bottoms used for cooking-up, syringes, loose belts, cotton swabs, and everything else a user uses to shoot up with. Naturally, I took my piece of dope and shoved it up into my rectum, and Chase did the same with his. We did our best not to move around too much while we did it. Cops look for that kinda stuff when they pull you over, and moving around frantically is probably the worst thing a person can do. They have no problem throwing on a pair of plastic gloves if they think you're hiding something "up there."

"Dude, I'm gonna run," Chase announced, glancing at me for approval.

"Hell no. Are you crazy? Just stay where you are, and stay cool. If you run, you're only gonna piss them off more. Just don't even think about it. Smile and say 'yes, sir.' That's all we can do now anyway."

I'd been through the drill enough times to know that I had to keep calm, but it didn't make a difference anyway. We didn't stand a chance. They tore Chase's mom's car apart and found everything but the dope, which pissed them off beyond comprehension, because they knew we had something stashed away—they simply didn't know where. Next, they lined us up next to one another and damn near strip-searched us on the side of the road, grabbing and shaking us like ragdolls to get the stuff to drop. Still, they found nothing. They even brought a K-9 to search the car, but they still couldn't find the H. Finally, outta desperation, they separated Chase and me and used every interrogation trick in the book to get one of us to break.

"Where is it? We know you have it—just tell us, and we'll let you go, alright? We'll say it was your buddy's, and you can walk off. How about it?"

Neither of us said a word. But even without the dope, they had enough gear piled away to arrest us, and that's exactly what they did. The car was repossessed, and we were dragged off to one of the grimiest institutions in St. Louis—Jennings County Jail. I was booked on possession of paraphernalia and a slew of outstanding parking tickets that had since turned into bench warrants. Chase got off easy with a single paraphernalia charge and was released not even an hour into being processed. I was so mad at him for leaving me in that place alone, but it wasn't his fault. It's just that I was starting to get sick already and wanted to spike my vein worse than ever. But I couldn't, so I did the only thing I could do without my tools. I squatted down, pushed the stuff outta my insides, and unwrapped it. I stuck it up my nose and tilted my head back to let it drip down my throat. The relief it brought me didn't last long, maybe a couple hours at the most.

I figured that my parents would come bail me out like they'd always done, but this time it was different. They wouldn't even accept my phone calls once they found out where I was and what I'd done. I was stuck, and every second in that place was worse than the one before. It stank like feces, and the cells were more suited for animals than they were humans. They kept the air conditioner on until it was almost freezing and gave us only a thin sheet to cover up with and a soiled pillow to lay our heads on. We were given soggy bologna sandwiches and room-temperature milk three times a day, and if you were lucky, you'd get an apple that wasn't half-rotten to chew around. Roaches darted from cell to cell scavenging for crumbs, and the little bastards would crawl on top of you when you were lying down and force you to jump up in the middle of the night and shake off.

The second day was the worst. Full withdrawal had taken effect, and I couldn't stop throwing up for the life of me. I was getting delirious, I couldn't sleep, and my insides felt like they were falling out. I went through an eight-hour period where all I did was scream and cry and beg until my throat was so sore that it hurt when I swallowed. My body temperature was going from extreme hot to extreme cold and then both at the same time. My skin started crawling and my flesh started burning and it felt like a billion little wasps were nesting inside of my stomach. The torture wouldn't stop though—it just got worse and worse, and time just got slower and slower. I tried to knock myself out by hitting my head against the concrete, but I didn't have the guts to keep going. I was so worn out afterwards that I pretty much just gave up and lay face down on the filthy concrete and prayed over and over for someone to come save me or kill me—I didn't care which at that point.

The guards would come around every few hours to check and make sure I was still breathing by poking me with their clubs through the bars until I made a noise. Sometimes, the nurse would come by and clean me off with a hot towel and force a cup of water down my throat and maybe a few bites of food. That was about it for medical care though.

When I heard my father's voice in the middle of the night on my second day, I thought I was hallucinating. It wasn't until I lifted my head up and saw him standing above me that I knew it was for real.

"Get your stuff, and let's go, Son."

I can't imagine how much it took outta him to see me like that. He held it together though. He held it together and held back tears and pulled me up off the ground and put his arm around my shoulder so tight that it hurt.

I pulled myself off the ground and walked outta the front door, and the midnight air hit me like a thousand BB pellets travelling at the speed of light. Hell is the best way to describe where I was at that moment.

"Dad?" I called out. "Dad, I need your help."

It wasn't long after that when I lost consciousness.

I came to my senses a day later. I could hear beeping in the background and could feel lines of liquid dripping into my veins. I opened my eyes and saw my mother staring out of a window across from me. She heard me moving around and ran over to me.

"Son, you awake?" she gently asked.

"Mom? Where am I?"

"You're at a hospital in Illinois. You've been here since yesterday detoxing, since after your dad picked you up from jail."

"Are you serious? I don't remember coming here."

"You were out of it, Son. You tried to jump out of the car, and your father had to tie you to the seat. They're taking good care of you here. Just sit back and relax, okay?"

"Okay, I love you, Mom. I love you so much."

"I know, and I love you too. We are going to get you better. I'm here now."

I couldn't hold back any longer. I cried like I was a baby again in my mother's arms. I cried for my mother. I cried for all the shameful things I'd done and all the nights I kept her up with worry. We cried together. She ran her hands through my hair, and I fell back asleep.

I remained at the hospital for another two days. The nurses woke me up every three hours to check my blood pressure and feed me pill cocktails—methadone for my withdrawals, clonidine for my anxiety, and about three other pills to keep my stomach in order and help me sleep. I was given 7.5 mgs of methadone on the first day, 5.0 mgs on the second, and 2.5 mgs on the last. I checked outta the hospital on the fourth day, still pretty out of it. It was the longest I'd gone without shooting up dope in almost a year. I felt things that I hadn't felt in so long—the soreness in my arms from shooting up, the sun on my back, the guilt and remorse in the pit of my stomach, the emptiness in my brain, and relief. I felt relieved for the first time in years, like I didn't have a million schemes running around in my head. I went home and took a long, hot shower to wash the grime away. I scrubbed every inch of my body as if I were scrubbing away my old life and creating a new one. I watched the water go down the drain and told myself that it was all the sickness and misery going away. I went downstairs to the kitchen and saw my mom cooking a meal for me—my first home-cooked meal in months.

"School starts in a week. I spoke to the principal at school, and they're willing to let you back for an extra semester to finish up. The only way they'll do it, though, is if you have your own personal escort everywhere you go. This is your last chance, and I urge you to take it. There's nothing else after this."

"No, no—I'll do it. Of course, I'll do it," I said without skipping a beat.

My mom looked surprised.

"Okay, perfect. I'm glad you want to finish. School's very important, and this can be your new beginning. It'll be your chance to show everyone who you really are."

"I won't let you down, Mom. I won't. I'm ready to be happy."

I scarfed down my food like a savage and ran upstairs to my room. I just wanted to sleep. I felt depressed. I felt lonely and abandoned. I didn't know what to feel. My feelings, once dulled by the prick of a needle, shot around in my head like an old, untamed gorilla. My feelings, and time, were my worst enemies. I had way too much free time on my hands and no hobbies or interests to fill it with. What the hell was I supposed to do with time? Normal stuff? Movies? Dinner? My mind was on the verge of exploding. I lit a cigarette to calm my nerves and tried not to think at all, but my head wouldn't leave me alone. I found the bottle of sleeping pills Dr.

Scott had prescribed me and threw about three of them into my mouth. Suddenly, my thoughts slowed down, my eyes got heavy, and I fell asleep.

I didn't know how I could ever live without drugs. The truth is I should never have gone home after detox. I should've run as far away from St. Louis as I possibly could've gotten and enrolled in some intensive inpatient treatment program and never looked back, but instead, I was thinking about finishing out high school and maybe going off to college. I just couldn't comprehend the fact that I wasn't like other people. I was an addict, and pretending like everything was okay was only gonna make things worse. I guess I wanted so badly to be like "them" that I never once thought that maybe I wasn't. When I finally realized that maybe I was a little different, it made me hate everyone even more. I hated them for being so damn content with the normal lull of life. I hated my friends for keeping it all together and leaving the prospect of going off to college open. I hated them for being and looking so happy when I was so sad.

Yet, despite my disdain for their joy, I secretly admired those who walked the path of normality. I admired the kid down the street who did all the right things and partied responsibly and got old and had a family and blah blah blah. I admired John and Jane Doe for waking up at dawn each day to legitimately provide for their families, putting aside selfish wants to fulfill their duties as husbands and fathers and wives and mothers. Everything they did was done in moderation and in good judgment, for the betterment of themselves or their family or those less fortunate. They contributed to society, paid taxes, donated money during the holiday season, voted on

Election Day, and drove to work each morning with nothing more than innocent thoughts of the upcoming weekend's plans and the following week's mortgage payment. Simple and uncomplicated were their thoughts, untouched by the familiar misery of my world and the headaches of an unrelenting and almighty addiction.

CHAPTER 8

GRADUATION/COLLEGE

I relapsed only two days after getting outta the hospital but still managed to graduate high school only a semester late. I swear my mom paid my teachers off or they just really wanted to get me the hell outta there, because I, in no way, deserved a diploma. Regardless, I left school and got a part-time job flipping pizzas at a pizzeria around the corner from my house. I also applied to a few junior colleges just to prove to my mother that I was actually trying to do something with my life. I was sure that there was no way in hell that a college would accept me given how piss poor my G.P.A. ended up being and how lengthy my disciplinary record was, but I was wrong.

About a month after I graduated from high school, a guy came by the house claiming to be a college recruiter. He told my mother and me that he was from a tiny college in a place called Fulton, Missouri, about two and a half hours to the south of St. Louis. The man went on to say that, although my grades were in the gutter, my ACT scores were good enough that they'd be willing to take a chance on me under very strict academic circumstances. Of course, my mom was overjoyed, and she told him "yes, yes, and yes" before I could get a word out, and as soon as he left, she was downstairs putting my clothes in a suitcase. It wasn't that she wanted me gone. I just think it was killing her to see me sitting around the house and doing nothing, and I'm pretty sure she knew I'd started using again.

A week before I left for school, my mom found a stack of needles under the sink in my bathroom on one of her daily searches. After she'd calmed down a lot, she and my dad came into my room for one last talk. My parents were just as worn down and worn out as I was from my habit. It was like a game of tug of war that never ended. They'd get a bit of leverage, and then I'd take it right back. Back and forth—every day—rain or shine, snow or sleet. Even my sister was beginning to show signs of distress from simply being around all of the commotion. The older she got, the more she began to understand what all the craziness was about, and the more she resented me for who I was and what I'd done to the family.

"So what now?" my mom asked, throwing the bag of rigs right beside me on the bed. "You're supposed to be going off to school in a week, and you're still doing the same crap. What are we supposed to do now?"

Normally, I would've done my best to convince them both that the stuff was old, but this time, I told the truth.

"I dunno. I still want to go to school. I'm not using because it's fun. I promise you that. I am using because I have to. Now that I'm gonna be far away from St. Louis, I think I have a better chance of staying clean, but first, I hafta get clean."

"But we just did that with you, remember?" my dad broke in. "You were just in the hospital for three nights."

"Yeah, but this is different. This time—this time, I actually want to get clean. I really do. Plus, this is really the only option we have if I still wanna make it to school."

I think I really was ready to get better, but I wasn't at all being fair to my parents or myself by assuming that detox was the golden ticket to curing my illness. Deep down, I knew that it wasn't. It was the easy way out though—the only short-term fix available at the time. So my dad forked over another five grand and checked me into detox for the second time in two weeks.

And just like all my previously failed attempts to get sober, that one was no different. Not only did I use each day leading up to detox, but all throughout it as well. As I sat in the hospital being pumped with methadone and Seroquel and a dozen other medications to keep me from getting sick, I shot heroin in the bathroom between nurse's visits for reasons I still can't explain. I don't know what the hell I was thinking or why I took dope with me to begin with. There was no reason to shoot junk—with all the tranquilizers and opiates they were feeding me, it would've been impossible to get sick. It was obvious that there was something seriously wrong with my head. Maybe Dr. Scott was right. Maybe it wasn't just a dependence issue. Maybe I was crazy—but I couldn't tell my parents that. They already had enough on their plate, and honestly, the truth would've destroyed them. They, at least, deserved to be hopeful.

I checked outta detox worse off than when I'd checked in. My life was in complete disarray. My habit had reached almost a hundred dollars a day, and counting—five shots in the morning, and just as many at night. Yet I went home that evening and wore a grand smile for my parents as we sat across from one another at the dinner table, talking about classes and what I planned on majoring in and how happy I was to finally be going off to school.

I left for college the next day with a couple grand in my bank account for schoolbooks, and food, and such and the keys to my brother's old Geo Prism. I said bye to my parents for what they thought would be the last time for a long time and headed two hundred miles south to a small town near the boot hill of Missouri where the two biggest attractions were a Super Wal-Mart and the state prison. My poor parents had no idea how easy they were making it for me. They'd given me enough money to keep me high for almost a month, and that was just with the upfront cash they'd thrown my way. But I thought I had it all figured out. I was sure that if I played my cards right, I could actually shoot dope and be a full-time student at the same time—like a functioning addict. I assumed that since I had money and didn't hafta spend all my time scrounging around, I could spend most of my days studying and going to class. I would just ration out my daily doses and only do enough to keep me from being sick.

But the one thing I didn't figure into my ingenious plan was how compulsive and outta control I was. I could ration out doses for days, but that wouldn't, and didn't, stop me from always doing and needing more than I set out to do. I also didn't take into account how clever my parents were by setting a limit on how much money I could withdraw from the ATM each day. So instead of making one, large trip to get everything, I was forced to make daily treks back and forth to St. Louis—three hours there and three hours back—just to keep from getting sick. Sometimes, I'd hafta go twice in a single day, and on more than one occasion, I spent the entire day in the car. My plan failed miserably, and within ten days of being at school, I'd blown through three quarters of my money stash and hadn't gone to a single class.

And to make matters even worse, my car stopped working a few days before I ran outta money, and I had to beg my roommate's girlfriend to run me to the city. I told her that it was an emergency and that I needed to go by my house to grab a check from my mom so I could purchase a much-needed schoolbook. She went along with it and drove me the entire way down, and when we arrived, I directed her to Shorty's place instead. I quickly ran in and grabbed what I needed and ran back out within seconds. She had no idea. On the way home, I had her stop by a gas station so I could use the bathroom. I grabbed a needle and my dope and bought a can of soda from the vending machine to cook up in. The damn lock on the bathroom door didn't work, so I stood up against it to keep anyone else from coming in. Right after pushing the plunger down on the needle, someone tried pushing the door open, and the needle broke off in my arm. Luckily, it was still halfway sticking out, so I snapped the thing out and quickly ran out to the car, wincing in pain.

I called my dad later that night and told him that I needed five hundred dollars to fix my car and another grand for school stuff. I don't know if it was my voice that sounded off, or if he just knew something wasn't right, but the very next day, he showed up at my dorm room doorstep on a mission to take control. I answered the door, of course not knowing it was him, and right when I saw him, I had a feeling that it was over for good. I knew he wasn't there just to say hi, and he wasn't—he'd already gone to the admissions building and verified that I hadn't attended a single class and was on the verge of flunking out.

"Get your stuff together. We're leaving in an hour," he said with a straight face.

"What do you mean 'we're leaving'?"

"I think you know exactly what I mean, Son. I already pulled you out of school, and all I want from you now is to listen very carefully to the words I'm about to say. If you aren't ready and in that car in an hour, I'm leaving, and you are to never have contact with anyone in this family for as long as you live. It's over. This is the end. If you want my help, you're going to do exactly as I say from here on out."

I didn't say another word. There was nothing to say, and in a way, I was relieved that it was over. My only concern was getting sick, but there was really nothing I could've done anyway—so I accepted my fate and forced myself forward. I got all my clothes and toiletries together and stuffed them in the trunk of my dad's rental car. Once we were on the road and I had nowhere to go, he told me that he was selling our house in St. Louis and getting a place a thousand miles away in Virginia and that I had no choice but to go with him.

"That's where we're headed now," he said. "No more Missouri. No more St. Louis. I'm moving the family to where I think it'll be safest, and right now, that place is Virginia. I have a job lined up in the city, and once you get yourself together, you can work, or go to school, or whatever. I don't care anymore. I honestly don't. Whatever's left in that house is getting tossed out after your mother and sister move up—so if you want anything, let your mother know, and she'll try and bring it."

"But what's in Virginia? I mean, I'm gonna get sick pretty soon, and we still hafta drive the whole way there, and then what? And what about my friends? I want to say bye to everyone."

"Well, I have a friend who's a doctor there, and he heads up a clinic that helps people like you. He told me to bring you in as soon we got in town and he'd give you some medicine to make you feel better. And Son, you don't have any friends. Your so-called friends are the ones who got you into this whole mess. You were a perfect child before we moved and they got ahold of you."

"Whatever, Dad. I did this to me. I did this to me, not my friends. What kinda medicine is the doctor gonna give me anyway?"

"I don't know. Just wait until we get there, and then you can ask him. I don't think you have any other options at this point."

I said nothing. It got dead silent, except for the sound of road outside.

"Look, there's something I have to tell you, and I want you to keep calm, okay? Can you do that for me? Keep calm?"

"Yeah, I guess. What is it, Dad? Just tell me already. I don't see how anything can be as bad as this right here."

"Jude," he paused between words. "Jude, I have cancer."

The words didn't sink in at first.

"Hold on; what?"

"I have cancer, Son."

I felt like I'd been stabbed in the stomach. Everything started to echo around and the wind outside the car got really loud and my father's voice faded into the background.

"I have cancer, Son. It's pretty aggressive. I was coming down to tell you next week, but when you called me, I could tell you needed me right away. Now, I need you. I need you like never before. Nobody else knows—just us. I don't want to tell your mom yet. Not until the house is sold and everyone is in Virginia and I talk to the doctor again about my options. Okay?"

I whispered 'okay' back, but it wasn't okay. I was crushed. I couldn't imagine life without my father. It was my fault that he was sick. It was definitely my fault. I'd put him through so much pain, unimaginable pain, the kinda pain that a person should never hafta feel—and it'd finally taken its toll. I deserved to be blamed. It was all my fault.

I needed a shot. I needed something to kill the awfulness I was feeling. I hated feelings. They were so strange to me. I hated them.

We drove for nearly an entire day in silence, taking turns every couple hundred miles and stopping off only to fill up on gas and eat. As the rest of whatever dope remained in my system metabolized and wore off, I got weaker and weaker and weaker. By the time we finally arrived at our hotel in Northern

Virginia, I was deathly sick and could hardly move. I pleaded with my father to take me to the hospital, but he told me to hold off and wait until the morning when we went to go see his doctor friend. I panicked. It was impossible to see an end to my agony. It felt like somebody had beaten me over every inch of my body with a sack of quarters. I just wanted it to end. I needed it to end. It had to end.

My dad dragged me into the elevator and up to our room on the fifth floor of our posh hotel. He laid me down on my side of the bed and covered me up with a horde of blankets to keep me warm. I was shivering like a wet dog.

My pleas turned into hysterical cries as the sickness got worse.

"Please, Dad, please take me to the hospital. Please. Why are you doing this to me? Why? I need help. Please take me."

"No, Son. No. Just a few more hours, okay? You can make it. I'm here with you. They aren't going to do anything at the hospital but give you drugs, and I honestly just don't have the money to go through that again. You've broken me, Son— financially and mentally and physically. But I'm here for you, and we are going to do it right this time. I'll be right here, okay? I promise."

We must've had that same back-and-forth conversation about going to the hospital five hundred times before the sun came up. I'd scream and beg for my father to take me, and he'd wipe the tears from my eyes and tell me to wait and hold off until the morning. The front desk people told us that if we didn't quiet down, they'd hafta ask us to leave. I tried my best to sleep, but I had that awful empty feeling that dope withdrawal leaves you with where you're uncomfortable in every position you try and you just wanna jump outta your awful skin and run away. I remember my dad combing his hand through my hair and tracing his finger behind my ears like my mom used to do when I was a kid to help relax me, but none of it worked. Lastly, I tied a bunch of socks around my arms in the places I shot up in most to get whatever dope might've been stuck in my veins to drain. I saw Markus do it a few times and figured anything would be better than nothing, but it didn't do a damn thing but make me wanna shoot up more. It wasn't until five in the morning that I finally wore myself out crying and screaming and I fell asleep.

My dad woke me up an hour later.

"It's time to get going, Jude," he said, leaning over me. "The clinic opens up in an hour, and they want you there right at seven. I brought you some coffee and a bagel from downstairs."

I opened my eyes.

"Jude?"

"Yeah, Dad. I'm awake. Just gimme a second, okay?"

"Sure, Son. Of course."

When I say that I woke up in a puddle of sweat, I don't mean it metaphorically. I literally woke up in a puddle of sweat. I stripped myself off the mattress and sat up. My dad had a wheelchair set up a few feet away from my bed that he wheeled over and helped me get into. It was the third day I'd gone without heroin and by far the worst day. I was completely broken, so broken that I couldn't even fight anymore. My dad just kept telling me that the doctor was gonna make it better, but I couldn't see better without heroin. I wanted just one more shot to chase the pain away. One more shot. One more rush. One more warm and cozy feeling. Just one more, and then I could rest.

I thought about running, but I was way too weak. I could barely even move my hands to itch the million scratches around my body. Plus, I was in an unfamiliar place and didn't have a dollar in my pocket. It would be damn near impossible to get high—not completely, but damn near.

We got to the clinic right on time. The place was nestled in a part of Northern Virginia known as Fairfax County. It was an area similar in most ways to St. Louis County but perhaps a little more racially integrated. Our hotel was only a stone's throw away from Washington, D.C. Actually, you could see the White House from our window, but I was in too much agony to care.

There was a line of people waiting outside the door when we pulled up—maybe fifty people or so. My dad helped me outta the car, and we got in line. I remember thinking to myself that it was a good sign that there were so many people there at the crack of dawn. I mean, they must've been doing something right to get everyone together that early. The clinic doors opened up right at seven, and the group flooded into the place like a herd of hungry cattle. There was really nothing to the waiting room but five or six wooden park benches, a couple cameras, and an intercom positioned above a heavy white door that led to the back area.

I signed my name on the sign-in sheet and told the person sitting on the other side of the tiny bulletproof glass window that it was my first day and I needed to see the doctor. I took a seat in the corner of the waiting room next to my dad and waited. The doctor showed up and introduced himself a few minutes later. He was stocky, bald, and short and reminded me a lot of George from Seinfeld, except he was Pakistani, not White.

"I'm Dr. Kashmiri. It's very nice to meet you, Jude. Your father has told me a lot about you," he said with a very thick accent.

"Oh yeah?" I mumbled back.

"Why don't we head back to my office and get you sorted out?"

"Both of us?" my dad interjected.

"No, just Jude for now, if you don't mind?"

"No, not at all. I'll just be out here."

I followed the doctor back to a small office and took a seat across from him.

"So Jude, what brings you here?"

"Basically, I'm sick. I haven't had heroin in three days now, and I'm really sick. I just need something to help me get through this."

"Okay. Well, do you know what we do here?"

"No."

"Well, we're what you'd call a methadone maintenance treatment program. Do you know anything about methadone?"

"Not really. I mean, I took it during detox a few times, but that's about it. It really helped a lot."

The doctor's words were like music to my ears. Methadone was like the next best thing for withdrawals. I even knew a few people back in St. Louis who used to shoot the stuff up when they couldn't get heroin. They said it took away the extended release part of the drug and made you feel it all at once. Of course, I wasn't planning on shooting up methadone, but it still made me feel more confident in the drug's abilities to know that junkies actually used the stuff to get high with.

"That's right," the doctor continued. "Methadone works miracles if it's not abused. Sure, it's an opiate, but so are painkillers. You wouldn't take a pain pill away from someone who has cancer, would you? You have a disease too. It's called addiction, and sometimes, the best way of treating that disease is with medicine. Now, if you were to enroll in our program, you'd have to come here every morning and take the methadone in front of a nurse until we feel comfortable enough to let you take it home with you. You must be in full compliance with the program to get 'take homes,' but if you come to group and individual counseling and pass all your drug screens, you'll do just fine."

"Well, I wanna do it. I wanna enroll today. I can't feel like this anymore."

I really couldn't. There's no telling what I would've done if I didn't get something to fix me.

"Okay, I'll need a urine sample from you, and your dad will need to pay a hundred dollars each week to keep you up to date with your payments. It's twenty dollars a day."

"Yeah, okay. I can do that."

"Now, the highest we can start you on is thirty milligrams. You can raise your dose by five milligrams each day, but that's it. That's the law."

"Thirty milligrams? Is that even gonna do anything?"

"Well, you'll still be a little uncomfortable, but yes, it will help immensely. How much were you using on the streets?"

"About a gram a day."

"Okay, well—you were pretty high up there. So it'll take a few weeks to get you on a comfortable dose. But once you're comfortable, you'll be able to lead a normal life again. You just have to be dedicated."

"I am—dedicated."

"Then let's do this. Here's the cup for the urine, and here's your patient number. Give this sheet to the receptionist, and she'll handle the rest."

"Thank you, Doctor. Thanks a lot."

I walked outta the room and took a seat on the benches in the waiting room while my dad paid the receptionist and took care of all the necessary forms. I looked around at all the different faces in the crowd—some were old, some were young, and some looked just as bad as me. There was even a pregnant lady there waiting to dose. Most everyone was talking, except for the youngest patients who stared at their phones most of the time. Every few seconds, the door would open, and someone new would come in. And every few seconds, someone's name would be called over the intercom, and they'd head back to the nurse's window to get their medicine. It was as orderly a system as I'd ever seen.

When my number was called, I got up, went to the back of the office, and greeted the nurse at the window. She grabbed a small disposable cup and put it under this crazy looking dispenser type thing. She typed thirty into the machine's keypad, and it shot out my exact dose a second later. The liquid was thick and red like cough syrup, just like the methadone I'd taken at the hospital twice before. She handed me the cup, and I gulped the stuff down and almost gagged. It was as awful as I'd remembered it being, like warm codeine cough syrup—but worse. I didn't feel anything at first, but I wasn't expecting to. Methadone takes about twenty minutes to kick in, and even when it does, you can't really tell. It's very gradual, not like heroin, where you loosen a belt and are immediately transported to a totally different place.

I walked outside and found my dad sitting on the hood of the car, staring off into the distance.

"I think this might work, Dad. I think it might actually work," I said, trying to feel him out.

"Well, I certainly hope so, Jude. Let me tell you something—if things don't work out with me, and I end up leaving you guys, it's going to be up to you to make things right, Son. I won't be here to save you anymore. This is it—the last lap. It has to work."

"You're gonna be fine, Dad. Please don't say that kinda stuff. Everything is going to be fine. You're not going anywhere, and I'm gonna make you proud. I won't let you down."

Something came over me, and I reached over and gave my dad a hug for the first time in probably four years. It was awkward at first, but after a minute, it felt right, and we were back to being old friends again. On our way back to the hotel, the medicine kicked in, and suddenly, I wasn't as sick. It didn't take all the symptoms away, but it damn sure made me feel hopeful again and gave me just enough of a boost to get me through the rest of the day.

I quickly adapted to the ways of the clinic and immersed myself in recovery. Every morning, I rose before nine and made the thirty-minute trek from our hotel room to the clinic where I received my tiny wax paper cup of meth syrup. I started going to group counseling every week and began living what most people would refer to as a "normal life." I even got a job at Starbucks and enrolled in classes at the local community college. I went to nightly Narcotics Anonymous meetings where I opened up to strangers who were just like me. I told them about all the awful things I'd done for drugs, most things anyway. And instead of hating me for it, they took me in like a second family and loved me even more for my faults. They had similar stories and came from similar backgrounds and had similar thoughts. For the first time, I didn't feel alone in my fight, and that was a relief.

My mom and sister joined my father and me in Virginia a while later, and the four of us settled down in a nice townhome about forty minutes outside of D.C. and fifty minutes from where my brother resided. Every Sunday, my mother would cook a feast big enough for an entire football team, and the five of us would sit across from one another at the dinner table like we'd once done. It was during our second dinner together that my father finally broke the news to everyone about his cancer. He'd already told my mom and me, but my brother and sister were clueless about the situation and reacted the same way I did when he first told me—disbelief and shock and anger, in that order exactly. I was almost positive that my brother and sister would find some way to blame me for my father's ailment, just as I blamed myself, but that never happened. On the contrary, actually—there wasn't a day that went by where someone in my family wasn't telling me how proud of me they were and how much they loved me and how good it was to see me alive again. There was still a lotta hurt and apprehension and skepticism, but for the most part, my family circled around me and gave me all the love and support I needed to keep going. It felt damn good, to be quite honest. Damn good.

I thought about home a lot. I thought about my friends, and I wondered if they missed me and if anything had changed since I was last there. I'd only been gone for a few months, but I was still only nineteen, and having a social life was still very much on my mind. It was just all so sudden; I'd gone from having a thousand friends in high school to none at all. I'd gone from an everyday twenty-four-hour routine to a Monday through Friday nine-to-five. I guess you could say I was lonely, lonely, and upset. I'd failed myself in so many ways. I should've been in school alongside everyone else, not community college, but a real university getting a real diploma and going to real college parties and football games and barbeques. It was hard not to beat myself up for all the lost opportunities. But I was alive—alive and sober and surrounded by people who loved me. I had to take what I could get.

I talked to Chase once or twice after leaving, but he was bitter and angry that I'd left and tried to sway me to come back every time. All I wanted was for him to be proud of me. I wanted him to say "good job" just one time, that's it—just one time—but I got nothing. He was still in an awful place anyway. He didn't come out and tell me that, but I knew Chase well enough to hear the gloom in his voice. All the liveliness had been sucked outta him and replaced by blackness—plain, awful blackness.

"Everything is falling apart, bro," he told me. "Stacy left me last week, and my parents kicked me outta the house and cut me off completely. I've been living with that fool Markus in that nasty apartment building we went to way back when. Remember the place you shot up in for the first time? Bill and Mandy's building or whatever?"

"No way, man," I responded, not knowing what else to say. "That's crazy."

"Yeah, it's all bad. After you left for college, I started shooting up, and things just went downhill from there. I just got outta rehab though. I'm getting off the stuff this time. I have to get Stacy back. I have to."

After getting off the phone with Chase for the last time, I had an awful feeling come over me, like it was the last time I'd ever speak to him again. It was as if I'd said goodbye to a ghost.

Most people will say that I just substituted one drug for another, and that may be true, but at the time—I didn't care. It was either die or get into a program like the one I was in where they gave you your fix but regulated it and made sure you were doing what you were supposed to do. And although people found ways to abuse the program, most everyone was there to get better. I mean, there were people who'd come in to grab their dose sporting thousand-dollar suits before heading off to work at some of the last places you'd imagine an addict working—law firms and hospitals and banks and government agencies. There were people who'd been on methadone for twenty-something years and who'd decided that they'd probably never get off and were completely content with it. Then, there were people like me—people who'd hit a brick wall and were just discovering the power of methadone and recovery for the first time. We were like infants just learning to walk—one step at a time, one day at a time.

CHAPTER 9

THE LIGHT

Sobriety came packaged with new challenges—new forms of mental torture to struggle with, new addictions to realize, and new habits to overcome. Things that I once did in moderation were becoming obsessions of mine—stuff like eating and sleeping and working and writing in my journal. I channeled my addictive nature into things that I thought were harmless, until I gained fifty pounds in two months and realized that maybe eating wasn't such a great thing to be compulsive about. So I turned to writing and working. I'd work all day at my new job at Starbucks and come home and write until three in the morning, or until I couldn't keep my eyes open anymore. I was so worn down half the time that I was hardly thinking straight, but at least I was staying busy. And staying busy was key. If I wasn't busy, then I was thinking, and if I was thinking, then I was more than likely thinking about bad stuff. Not bad stuff like getting high but bad stuff like all the emotions that were hitting me at once. There was guilt and remorse and anger and sadness and more guilt stacked on top of more guilt. There were new feelings and then old feelings and then fake feeling and real feelings. It was especially hard, because I'd always suppressed every emotion that came my way with drugs, and suddenly, I didn't have that to rely on anymore. I had to face everything the natural way—head on and without anything to numb me. Let's just say that my moods were erratic a lotta the time. One moment I was laughing, and the next I was crying. One moment I was upset, and the next I was happy. I was all over the place.

Perhaps one of the worst habits that'd carried over from my old life was my inability to tell the truth. I lied about everything and anything when there was absolutely no reason to at all. I'd leave the house at eight but tell my parents I'd left at seven. I'd get a B in class but tell my parents I'd gotten an A. I'd eat vegetable soup for lunch but tell everyone I had chicken. I was telling people what I assumed they wanted to hear instead of what was right and honorable—the truth. In most ways, I was still living like an addict—still looking over my shoulder and preparing for something awful to happen. I even held onto a bag of syringes I'd brought with me from St. Louis. It was like a security blanket of sorts. It was as if I was ready to relapse. I'm pretty sure I expected it.

But not everything was all bad, not by a long shot. Aside from all the emotional drama and all the lonely nights, I often reveled in my new way of life. My arms were healing, and the dark dope circles around my eyes had lightened to a shallow tint. I was finally beginning to feel like life was maybe worth living without drugs, like maybe the normal lull of a nine-to-five existence wasn't so bad after all.

I was so ashamed of the person I'd become when I was getting loaded that I decided to never set foot on Missouri soil ever again, no matter what. There were just too many bad memories there for me to ever feel like going back was worth it. Everything back home reminded me of getting high anyway. My counselors called them "triggers."

"Anything can be a trigger for you, Jude," one of them told me once. "It can be something as simple as a billboard or as recognized as the St. Louis Arch. It could be highways or rivers or street signs or old homes. You can't control them either. It just happens, and for now, you're not strong enough to overcome those feelings. Just leave it alone. This is your home now, Jude. This is your home."

They were right. I had to put Missouri outta my mind. I had to put everything outta my mind. I had to forget and create new memories and create new friends—good friends. I took it even ten steps further and created an entirely new persona. In this alter persona, I'd already graduated college and I loved to hike and camp and read and I'd never done a drug more harmful than marijuana in my life. Every time someone at work would ask me about my past, that's the one I gave them. If there was a way I could've erased my old memories, I probably would've done it in a second. I didn't wanna remember anything.

Plus, there was already so much going on with my dad and his cancer that it seemed only right to put my demons on the backburner and focus on him for a while. I still went to group and the clinic every day and stayed off everything but methadone, but I guess you could say that I made my recovery less of a priority than it was when I first got off dope.

My father's health was deteriorating faster than anyone could keep up with. It'd been a year since he was diagnosed with cancer, and the tumor on his pelvis hadn't done anything but get bigger. The doctors were too scared to operate on him, because they said it was "too risky" of a procedure, since the affected area was in a place that was flooded with blood vessels and arteries. So, instead, they pumped him full of so much chemotherapy and radiation that he lost almost half his weight and all of his hair and just about every muscle on his body after only a few treatments. The worst side effect, though, were the hiccups. He'd get them for hours, sometimes days at a time, without a break. The poor man would be sitting there trying to eat, and he'd get the hiccups, or he'd be sleeping, and he'd get the hiccups, or talking, and he'd get the hiccups. It was nonstop, and it wore him down more than anything else.

I spent the next nine months by my father's side—in the hospital and in the basement of our home. I started up a saltwater fish tank and spent almost every dime I was making at work loading it with exotic fish and coral reef from the ocean. I set it up only a foot away from my father, so he could see me at all times and know that I was there for him whenever he needed me. I guess he started feeling like his life was slipping away, because he started talking to me like it was always the last time.

"We've been on a long journey together, you and I. I know we haven't had much of a relationship lately, because of everything that's gone on, but you have to know that I love you more than anything in this world, and I am so, so proud of you, Son."

"I know you are, Dad. I know that. But you hafta stop talking like you're not gonna make it. You're gonna be fine. You hafta be fine. I won't let you leave us, Dad. I won't."

And then there were times when my dad was so hiked up on meds that he'd only get out a sentence or two before passing out. He was in so much pain, but he fought it with everything in him so we didn't hafta see him hurt. He didn't let us know half of what he was feeling inside, and he was adamant about doing the things he'd always done, like bathing and eating and changing, all on his own. He was too proud to let anyone help him. There were times, though, when he couldn't hold it in, and I'd hear him whimpering through the walls like a kid who was sick with the flu. At first, I'd just put a pillow over my head and cry my eyes out until I fell asleep, but then it got really bad, and my hair started falling out from the stress, and I started falling apart.

I was on the verge of having a complete mental breakdown. Of course, I didn't tell anyone how I was feeling inside, because I didn't want anyone thinking any less of me, and I didn't wanna take any attention away from my dad. So I held it in for as long as I could until I couldn't anymore, and then, well, then I relapsed.

CHAPTER 10

The Fall

I could use my dad's condition back then as an excuse for why I started smoking weed again, but the simple fact is that I put myself in a very vulnerable place at a very vulnerable time and screwed away an entire year of sobriety. The moment I put my recovery on the "backburner," I made an unconscious decision to relapse. I justified my using by telling myself that as long as I didn't use heroin, I was still technically clean, but we all know that's bullshit. I was an addict. It didn't matter if it was heroin or marijuana or speed. Eventually, they'd all take me to a bad place, because I had no self-control. I was immoderate in the worst way.

I didn't tell anyone that I'd started smoking again—not even my mom or my counselors at my clinic knew. The only people who knew that I was getting high for sure were the people who sold me the stuff, but they didn't know enough about my past to think that it was a problem, and I wasn't about to tell them. They were just some guys I'd met at work who liked to smoke pot and sold a bit on the side as well. They'd asked me a bunch of times before to hang out, but it wasn't until things got really bad with my old man that I finally gave in and went against my better judgment and decided it was time to get away. I needed a release.

I didn't even make it ten minutes into my first outing with the guys before I put that first blunt up to my lips and shit away my sobriety like it was nothing. I felt a tremendous amount of guilt after the high wore off, but then I just got high again, and it went away like magic. It was a vicious cycle—guilt and remorse followed by an unrelenting high, guilt and remorse followed by an unrelenting high—and over and over again like a broken record.

But my downward spiral didn't stop there. I took it a hundred steps deeper and began pinching pills—oxycontin and morphine mainly—outta my father's medicine chest to keep up my inner demons at bay. My parents kept them outta sight in the beginning, but as time went by and things got more hectic around the house, they stopped caring as much about hiding pills and spent their time on more pressing issues, like medical bills and what to do with this and that in case my father did die. Taking my dad's cancer pills was probably one of the more shameful things I ever did. I'd smile right in the old man's face and then tiptoe behind him to where his pills were and shake a few into my mouth. Methadone took away most of the euphoric effects, but that wasn't why I was taking them anyway. They numbed me. They murdered my thoughts and feelings and helped me sleep at night. They took away my anxiety and put the hair back on my face. They made me feel normal.

As the days went by, I began spending less and less time at home and more and more time with my work buddies, James and Trent and Tracy. They were all probably around my age, twenty or so, but dressed like they were still in high school—baggy jeans, and hoodies, and backwards hats, and such. Tracy, their self-proclaimed leader, reminded me a lot of a guy I used to know back in St. Louis—a guy I used to shoot up with. They had the same stupid permanent smirk plastered across their face, amongst other things—same chiseled-down nose, same boxed-up cheekbones, same mashed-up eyebrows, and the same cold, green eyes.

I smoked pot nonstop for a whole month before I started selling it. It started with a couple of dime bags here and there and progressed into halves and ounces pretty quick. Before I even had a chance to plant my feet and figure out what the hell I was doing, I was selling so much weed for Tracy that it was almost impossible to keep my day job. I don't really know how it happened—it just did, ya know. We got to talking one day, and he asked me if I wanted to make some money, and I said yes—that was it.

I had no idea what I'd gotten myself into. Tracy might've seemed like a nice enough guy, but in reality, he was an unforgiving, self-serving wannabe thug with a chip on his shoulder and a thirst for power. He only worked to wash his money, and he washed his money because most of it came from drug sales—hence why he wanted me selling for him. The cops were on his ass big time, and it'd almost become impossible for him to move product anymore, so he had everyone else do it for him. Of course, I didn't know any of this at the time. It took months before I figured out that his real name wasn't even Tracy—it was Boyd or something.

I sold Tracy's pot around the clinic and at school, and within a week, I was selling quarter pounds for the kid and making a pretty penny doing it. I could feel myself slipping deeper and deeper back into my past. I just kept telling myself that I'd do things differently the next time around and then the next time around, but then the next time would come around and nothing would change. My dad was at home dying, but all I could think about were my needs and my wants and my desires. I was selfish. I was delusional. I was a wimp— an escape artist. The second I started feeling the least bit bad, I'd just pop another pill or smoke another blunt or increase my methadone dosage at the clinic to numb me even more. I guess I just hadn't hit rock bottom yet—the point where you're so low to the ground that you'd do anything to get back up and the very thought of using again seems like suicide. But maybe that's exactly what I needed to get better. Maybe I deserved everything that was coming to me, and then some.

CHAPTER 11

DAY OF SHOVELS AND BATS

The worst day of my life came a few months later on a bright and sunny day in the summer of another lost year. I was sitting comfortably in the basement of my house spending a few minutes of valuable time with my father when my phone rang.

"Hey, Jude. I'm out here by your car. I need your help with something."

It was Tracy. I paused for a second and ran upstairs to look out the window. They were all out there—Tracy, James, and Justin—standing directly in front of my house like a bunch of hoodlums straight outta an Eminem music video. It didn't make sense that they knew where I lived—I'd never taken them by my house, not ever. I hung up the phone, made sure my mom wasn't around, threw on a hoodie and a pair of shoes, and slipped outside as quietly as I could.

"Yeah, what is it?" I inquired, trying my best to hold back my anger.

"You alright, man?" Tracy asked, stepping forward.

His eyes were cold and evil.

"No, not really. You can't just come by my house and expect me to jump. People around here are already watching me, and my dad's in there sick as hell, and my mom's falling apart. How did you know where I live, anyway?"

"Come on, bro. You think I'd be giving you all this weed on consignment and not make it my business to find out where you live? It's what I do. And I'm sorry about coming by like this. It's important though."

"Okay, well we can't talk out here. I don't want my mom seeing us."

"You wanna take a ride then? We can run down the street," Justin interrupted, pointing to his car.

"Sounds good."

We jumped into Justin's car and sped off, and Tracy lit a blunt and started passing it around. We pulled into an empty lot a few blocks away from my place and parked.

"Basically, I'm gonna tell you like this," Tracy said. "We need your help getting James's watch back from a friend's house. It's a long story, but in short, James owed this kid, Trent, some money, so he gave him his watch as collateral. James paid Trent back, but Trent doesn't wanna return the watch. So we decided we're gonna mob over to his place and take it back, no matter what."

"Is this the same Trent you get your weed and stuff from?" I asked.

"Yeah, it is. That's why we've waited so long, or else we would've gotten it back a long time ago. I didn't wanna mess things up with him."

I was confused.

"Alright, so what do you guys want with me?"

"Well, now that you're part of the crew, I figured you'd wanna ride with us. We all look out for one another, you know?"

"Yeah, I hear you. But look, I've been doing a lotta thinking lately, and I think it's time I take a little break from everything—smoking and selling and everything. I just wanna be there for my dad while I can, you know?"

Tracy stared at me blankly. He seemed disappointed.

"He's probably gonna die soon, and I need to be there for him. He's always been there for me, so I kinda feel guilty about always being gone. You can understand that, right?"

"Yeah, actually I can. My mom died of cancer."

He stared down at the floor for a moment and crossed his chest and pointed to the sky.

"What about now though?" he answered back.

"Now?"

"The thing with Trent?"

Tracy pulled a gun out from under his pants and set it on the dash. It threw me off completely.

"I mean, I guess I can go over there with you guys."

Tracy shook his head in approval.

"That's what I'm talking about. See, I told you guys Jude would be down."

And that was the last of it, or actually, the beginning. It's amazing how one spontaneous decision can change your life forever.

In the car ride over to Trent's, Tracy rehearsed the plan out loud and made sure everyone knew what to do.

"So, James and I are gonna go in, and everyone else is gonna hang back in the car. He thinks we're coming over to pick up some weed, but he'll probably think something's up if we all go up there at once. The only way you guys get outta the car and come inside is if one of us calls you. That shouldn't happen though; I'm pretty sure he'll just hand over the watch. Everyone good with the plan?"

"Yeah," the rest of us rang out.

"Alright, let's do this then."

We pulled into Trent's neighborhood a few minutes after noon and parked a few streets over from where his actual house was located. Tracy and James hopped outta the car and headed to the trunk, where they grabbed out a bunch of garden tools—a shovel and an ax and weed whacker type thing—before disappearing into the woods right behind what I imagined was Trent's place.

I assumed they were gonna use the stuff to scare Trent with. It never occurred to me, not for a second, that they might actually use the stuff on him.

Minute after minute ticked by as Justin and I sat in the car waiting for any sign of their return. I knew something was up, but I tried my best to keep calm. The last thought that ran through my head right before the phone rang was *God, please don't let that phone ring*. Then, the phone rang, and I knew right away that it was Tracy or James calling to order us inside.

"Come on—we need you in here," James said in a calm but nervous tone over the phone's loudspeaker before hanging up.

There was a dark silence behind his voice. He sounded indecisive and troubled yet composed all at the same time. My mind raced, my heart dashed, and my nerves jumped. There's nothing I wouldn't have given at that moment to simply disappear, but that wasn't gonna happen, so I did the next best thing and slapped on one of my father's fentanyl patches that I had tucked away in my pocket all along. It calmed me down instantly.

"Yo Jude, you with me?" Justin asked as he threw a ski mask over his face and a pair of black gloves over his hands.

"Yeah, I'm here. I'm with you—just trying to collect my thoughts."

The two of us got outta the car and started walking toward the house. It was broad daylight outside, and I was sure that someone was gonna see Justin in his ski mask and call the police, but the neighborhood was dead. My stomach fluttered with anticipation as I moved quickly to the edge of the yard and through the back patio door with Justin right in front of me. Immediately upon entrance into the house, I could hear a baby's cries coming from the den followed by muffled screams and, finally, crying. We walked to where the noise was coming from, and that's when I saw all of them on the floor, all three of them—a baby, a woman, and Trent. It was as if all the worst of my conjured-up fears were unfolding right before me in a dream-like sequence from hell: James was in my peripheral holding a twenty-two-caliber pistol to the back of Trent's neck while Tracy stood above the woman and child with a bat draped across his shoulder like he was preparing to take a swing. Trent looked helplessly around the room with a look of defeat and betrayal in his eyes. It was scary how much he looked like my old friend Chase—skinny and tall and very white with ocean-blue eyes and blond hair and a square jaw.

"You guys are supposed to be my friends!" he screamed. "You owed me that damn watch for the weed you never paid me back for. What the hell did you expect?"

"Trent, I swear if you say another word—you're getting one in the head," James announced, sliding back the shaft of the gun to get a round in the chamber. "You're giving me an effing headache. Last time—where's the watch?"

"*Alright, dammit*—it's upstairs in my drawer. Take me upstairs, and I'll get it for you."

"Alright, let's go upstairs then. But if you make one wrong move, you're finished and your kid is finished and your girl is done. Don't think I won't shoot you, Trent."

The whole time this is going on, I'm standing off to the side in complete shock and disbelief. I'd thrown my hood up over my head, but most of my face was still showing. I didn't know what the hell else to do. It was beyond anything I'd ever been involved in and anything I'd ever imagined being involved in. The rest of the guys seemed to be getting some sadistic kick outta the situation, like it was entertainment to them or something.

Everyone went upstairs right behind Trent except me. I stayed downstairs with the mother and child. The lady was hysterical by that point. She was holding that baby so close to her chest that I was sure she'd suffocated it.

Suddenly, all this noise started coming from right above us, and the entire house was overcome with violent screams of torture and pounding so loud that the chandelier shook above me, the drywall cracked beside me, and the floor vibrated beneath me.

"What are they doing to him?" the lady screamed out. "They're gonna kill him."

"Trust me, nobody's gonna hurt him. We're just here for the watch, is all. I promise, nobody's gonna get hurt. Everything's gonna be alright. I won't let anything happen to you."

In reality, though, I had no worldly idea what they had planned. The situation was completely outta my control. I was getting anxious. I screamed upstairs to hurry them along, but it just got loud again, and the baby started crying, and I didn't know what the hell to do.

I grabbed a rattle from across the room and handed it to the baby, and she calmed down a bit, but not much. I started pacing around the room like a zoo animal to pass time. A minute passed, and then another and another. The noise was overpowering: screaming, pounding, and crying. And then finally, after five minutes, James, Tracy, and Justin came galloping down the stairs with half-empty black garbage bags by their sides. Trent was nowhere around.

They were all laughing and whispering to one another about this and that and the other. For all I knew, Trent was dead, and they'd chopped his body into tiny parts and thrown him in the trash bags beside them. There was blood splattered across James's shirt, and especially across Tracy's pants—even his shoes had large spots of blood pasted across them.

They exited the house, one by one, and I soon followed. Before I went outside, though, I turned to Trent's girlfriend and gestured a quiet apology using only my lips. I put my head down and followed the three of them through the sunlit suburban block to James's car. There was so much I wanted to say and so much I wanted to ask. I wanted to know what was in the bags and what they did to Trent and why there was blood on their clothes and why things happened the way they did to begin with. More than anything, I needed to know if Trent was okay.

"So what the hell just happened? Did you guys get the watch, or what?" I finally said, after we'd all settled into our respective seats in the car.

Tracy laughed and cleared his throat before opening up one of the bags and pulling out a thick stack of hundred-dollar bills, a few Saran-wrapped bricks of pot, and a cocaine-filled Tupperware canister. James's watch was the last to appear, a petty gold-plated scrap of metal that was quickly tossed back into the bag with complete irrelevance and disregard. That's when it finally occurred to me that it was never about the stupid watch. They'd taken me in there with every intention of robbing the kid. I was angrier than ever, but I didn't say a word. They had the gun, not me.

"What's up with Trent?"

Tracy stared at me blankly before answering.

"Trent? Well, I guess he's alright. I'm sure he's got a few bumps and bruises, but he'll survive. The gun wasn't even loaded, by the way—but it sure as hell worked like it was."

Everyone laughed, and I forced a smile, and we all agreed to meet back up at Tracy's place later on in the evening to divvy up the stuff and figure out what our next move was gonna be in case Trent decided to retaliate. I went home and ate dinner with the folks, and when six o'clock came around, I forced myself over to Tracy's house. I was already in so deep that there was no backing out. If Trent came looking for them, he'd definitely come looking for me too. Also, if I didn't show that night, they would've just shown up at my house same as before. There was no way out.

All the usual suspects were already there, shooting pool and sipping off a champagne bottle.

"Yo, Jude!" Tracy exclaimed upon seeing me. "Nice that you can join us. We put together a little present for you. Go take a look."

I walked over to where Tracy was gesturing to and stopped dead in my tracks when I saw it all there laid out. It was all there—everything we'd taken from Trent divided into four neat piles.

"This is for me?" I asked.

"Yeah, bro—one of them is, at least. You're one of us now. It's all there: two pounds of green, an ounce of coke, and five grand cash. We're all in this together."

"Tracy, this is too much, man. You know I appreciate this more than anything, but I really do need to spend more time with my old man. He's really sick, and he needs me."

"Okay, but this is different, because this is your stuff, not mine. There's no payment deadlines or anything like that. You can spend time with your pops and sell whenever you want, you see? It works out for everyone."

I had to take the stuff. I had no choice. It was Tracy's way of making sure every one of us shared the same amount of guilt and burden and blame in his sloppy heist. It was his insurance, so to speak.

"Alright, man. Thanks, Tracy," I finally replied.

"No problem, bro. I take care of my own, you see?"

"What about Trent? You think he'll come after us?"

"Hell no," James broke in. "He knows who we are. He knows not to mess with us, and what's he gonna do anyway— call the cops and tell them we went over there and stole a bunch of drugs from him? Hell no. Think about it."

"True. Alright, well, what now?" I asked, irritated by James's tone.

Tracy picked up a bottle of champagne and poured each of us a glass.

"I'll tell you what now," he announced. "Now, we reward ourselves. We invite some girls over, and we party. But first, let's toast. Let's toast to us—The Crew—the most loyal group of guys I've ever known. Nothing will ever tear us apart, nothing."

For the next couple of days, I stuck around the house and helped my mom out with chores related to my dad—feeding and keeping him company, mostly. No news had come through the pipeline about Trent, but the way I figured it—no news was good news.

And then, the shit hit the fan like never before, and the worst thing imaginable happened—James was arrested for his part in the home invasion. I was at the hospital picking up more prescriptions for my dad when I got the dreaded news from Tracy over the phone. He was frantic, and I could tell that something really bad had happened. He just kept saying, "Jude, it's over," over and over and over again. I just assumed Trent had finally come around and done something vengeful.

"What is it, man?" I asked. "You're freakin' me out."

"We're all done, Jude. James just got arrested up at work for the Trent thing. Everyone's saying Trent gave us all up, man. Trent gave us up. And even worse than that, he's in effing hospital on life support. Dude, if he dies—we're all going in for murder."

"Wait, but Trent doesn't know me. If the cops show up at my door, that means James gave me up, not Trent. He wouldn't do that, would he?"

"No, man. James would never do that. He's a standup kid. I've known him since we were small. He would never talk."

Tracy didn't sound very reassuring when he spoke, and the more Tracy spoke, the more I wanted to die. All the blood in my body rushed into my head, and my breathing got heavy. I lost it.

"I didn't touch that kid, not once. Why the hell am I getting dragged into everything? I never should've gone over there with you, man. I told you that he wasn't gonna just take this lying down, didn't I? And now he's in the hospital on life support? You said he was fine when we left."

"Look, it got a little outta hand upstairs, and we might've hit him over the head with the gun. When we left, though, he was just bleeding a little, not much. I thought he was gonna be okay. It doesn't matter now. What matters is that we all stick together and stay calm."

"You might've hit him over the head? Might've? You little punk—you guys were planning on robbing him all along, weren't you?"

"Jude, calm the hell down. Seriously. Remember who you're talking to."

"Yeah, I'm talking to an idiot. You think I'm scared of you? You're a punk."

"You sure about that?"

"Yeah, I'm damn sure. Go to hell, Tracy."

I hung up the phone, ran into an empty bathroom at the hospital, and screamed my head off for a straight minute. I found an empty room to reflect in and sat there for an hour, or more, just staring at the wall. I was so mad at Tracy, but I was mad at myself even more. For the hundredth time in my life, I'd gone against my conscience and set myself up for a major fall. I had nobody to blame but myself though. Nobody made me go into that house. Nobody made me start smoking pot again. It was all me. It was all me in the beginning, and it was all me in the end.

I was positive that James was gonna give us all up, if he hadn't already. The streets are funny like that. Everyone is always so loyal to one another until they get popped and are all of a sudden facing decades in prison. Then, it's just a race to see who testifies against whom first. I knew James would flip, because they'd thrown the book at him just to make sure he did just that. The charges leveled against him were deep and costly—malicious wounding by a mob, two counts of abduction, one count of robbery, and a fifth, and final, felony charge for the firearm. Each felony count carried a minimum of five years in prison and a maximum of twenty or so. It didn't take a genius to predict that he'd say just about anything to save himself.

Since the house was in my parents' names, I knew that the police, if and when they came, would only have a warrant for my room, which is where I kept everything to begin with. There was just way too much stuff to take a chance anyway, so I threw everything incriminating I could find in a box and sealed it for good measure. I got most of the major stuff out, like the gun and leftover coke and pot, but I didn't want it to be suspiciously clean, so I left a few cannabis seeds lying around and called it a day. I put the box downstairs in the basement and threw a bunch of other boxes on top to make it look like it'd been there for a very long time. There was nothing left to do but wait.

Monday came and went, and nothing. Then, Tuesday and Wednesday came—still nothing. It wasn't until Thursday, a full four days after James was arrested, that they finally came pounding down my door. I'm sure my mom would've opened the door for them if they'd asked, but instead, they chose to knock the thing off its hinges and toss a flash bang grenade into the house, just barely missing my bed-ridden father. There were twenty of them, all dressed in black riot gear with masks covering their faces.

I wasn't home, of course, but my mom later told me that it sounded like a bomb had gone off and she thought they were being attacked. My dad barely weighed a hundred pounds at the time and looked just as sick as he was, but even he wasn't immune to their violent treatment.

"Where's your son? Where's Jude," they screamed after concluding that I, indeed, was not home.

They had everyone in my family circled together around the kitchen table as they pounded them with question after question regarding my whereabouts.

"We honestly don't know," my sister answered. "We don't know where he is."

My mom was too panic-stricken to answer anything, and my father was breathing so hard that they had to call over a medical team to make sure he was okay.

"I'm sorry, but I don't believe you. I don't believe that you don't know where Jude is. Does he have a cell phone?"

"Yeah."

"Then maybe we should try and call him? How about it?"

"Can you tell us what he did first? This hasta be some sort of a mistake. Jude is better now. He doesn't do bad stuff anymore," my mom broke in.

"Look, Ma'am. We have an arrest warrant for your son, Jude Hassan, and a search warrant for his room. I don't know anything else about the situation. My job is to find Jude and bring him in. When the detectives get here, then you can ask them what this is all about."

As if on cue, a heavyset detective stepped forward with a bagged and tagged Hi-Point pistol in his right hand, the same Hi-Point pistol we'd used to rob Trent with. His tranquil demeanor was a comforting reassurance to my parents, although the gun kinda threw them right back into panic mode.

"Do any of you know what I'm holding here?" he asked, signaling my mom for an answer.

"No, of course not. Why would we? What are you saying? Please, just tell me what this is all about!"

"I'm getting to that part, Ma'am. The reason I'm showing you this gun is because this is the gun Jude and his friends used to rob and beat a kid nearly to death almost a week ago today. You're telling me you know nothing about this?"

"Oh my God. Are you serious?" my mom asked, holding her hands up to her mouth as tears began to fall from her tired eyes.

"Unfortunately, yes. It isn't all bad though. His role was quite limited in this whole thing. We've already spoken to one of the kids involved, but we need to hear Jude's side of the story. Right now, all he can do is turn himself in so we can get this whole thing cleared up," the detective said, gesturing toward a cell phone on the table. "Call him, and see if he'll come home, but don't tell him we're here or else he won't show up."

My mom grabbed the phone and dialed my number. I didn't answer. She called five more times before I finally picked up.

"Jude, Son—I need you here at the house. Can you come home, please?"

I was immediately suspicious. There was something about my mom's voice that scared me to death.

"Why, Mom? What happened? Is it something with Dad?"

"No, Son—it's not your dad. We just need you here."

"Is someone there?"

She was silent.

"Are the police there?"

Silence.

"Look, if they're there, just say my name once."

"Jude."

I hung up and powered off my phone. I'd anticipated that moment for four long days, but there was no amount of anticipation or readiness that could've prepared me for the immediate feeling I got when it actually happened. My life literally flashed before me in an instant, and the realization that I hadn't done a single good thing in my life hit me like a freight train. I was a bad person, and I'd been a bad person for a very long time. I was selfish and ungrateful and deceitful and, above all, a bad son. I'd held my family ransom for six very long years. I'd turned my parents into shadows of themselves, no longer able to even force a smile anymore or think about the past without blaming themselves in some way for what went wrong. I was more than a bad son; I was a horrible person.

There were three new voicemails on my phone when I turned it back on, all from this guy claiming to be a detective outta the Police Department. His voice was stern and loud, like my father's once was before he got sick.

"Jude," the message began. "This is Detective Prier with the Violent Crimes Unit. Jude, we have a serious situation here, and I really need to speak with you about it. We're leaving your house now, but we'll keep coming back if you force us to. Jude, just do the right thing and turn yourself in, okay? I've left my card with your parents, so when you get home, I urge you to give me a call. Okay. Bye."

I'd already made the decision to turn myself in, but I wouldn't do it without a lawyer by my side. There was no telling what James had told the cops to get them to come to my house first, but it didn't really make a difference. We were all going down together. Just like Tracy had said, we were all in it together.

I settled in for the night at a hotel down the street from my house, and when morning came, I acquired the most reputable defense attorney I could afford and retained his services for a cool ten thousand dollars—two grand for each felony count against me. Afterwards, I went to the clinic and drank my daily dose of methadone and called my mother to meet somewhere and talk before I turned myself in.

We met at a small café in between our house and the County Courthouse. I didn't even recognize her when she walked in. Her face was heavy with burden, and her eyes were puffed out from crying. It looked like she'd aged fifty years since I'd last seen her. She came and took a seat across from me at a table in the corner.

"Shame on you for what you have done to us," she whispered, her voice getting progressively louder. "Shame on you for taking advantage of our kindness and our love. Shame on you for making us feel guilty and for making us feel like bad parents. We have done everything for you. Everything—and this is how you repay us? You are no longer my son. You are not the boy I raised. You are someone else."

"Mom, please."

"No, you don't have the right to call me that anymore."

"Mom, look—I'm sorry, okay? I'm sick. Something is wrong with me. I don't know what happened to me either. I'm sorry it's come to this."

"No, you're weak. You're weak. That's what you are."

"Fine, I'm weak. I'm weak and I'm sick and I'm a horrible person. I'm an awful son and an awful person. I'm probably gonna spend the rest of my life in prison now, because I followed a bunch of idiots into a house for no reason."

I put my head down and started crying. The seriousness of the situation I'd gotten myself into was all coming to the surface and busting me up at the seams.

"I don't know what happened to me, Mom. I used to be so happy, remember? Everyone used to love me, and now look at me—I'm nothing."

I was laughing and I was crying and I was embarrassed and then angry. I could feel and see everyone staring at me as if I were an act in the circus or something. I threw my hands up in the air and started wailing like a maniac.

"I hate you all! I hate you all!" I screamed before my mom rushed me outside.

I had officially hit the wall. My mom put me into her car and slammed the door shut. It was time to go. The detectives were waiting. Prison was waiting.

CHAPTER 12

HELL: THE CELL

I t was five minutes after seven when my mother, Lawyer Gibbons, and I entered the courthouse for the first time. The marble-laden building stood tall with magnificent and intimidating strength—its large, Romanesque statues were a sobering reminder of the larger-than-life problems that afflicted me. My mom held me tight as we walked, afraid that I'd have another meltdown or maybe try and run.

"Take off your belts, and turn in your cell phones," one of the sheriffs announced as he handed us an empty plastic tub to put our metals in. "Shoes and belts off. Turn your cell phones in at the desk."

My mother, my lawyer, and I got in line behind a hundred or so other people and made it through to the other side with about forty minutes to spare.

"So, why don't we go through everything before we meet with the detectives?" my lawyer, an affable guy with grey slicked-back hair and piercing green eyes, suggested.

"Yeah, okay," I replied, wiping my sweaty palms off on the side of my pants for the twentieth time. "Okay."

The three of us sat down on the first open bench we could find and began preparing for the end of my world as I knew it.

"Well, I think it's safe to say that these guys have done their homework. They have a slew of evidence against all four of you, and especially you, Jude. It looks like James's claiming that this was all your plan and they were just along for the ride. Between you and me, though, Detective Prier doesn't believe any of it. He's already spoken to the victims, Trent and his girlfriend, and they did say that you were downstairs the whole time and were actually trying to hurry everyone out. Is that true?"

"Yeah, that's pretty much what happened."

"Well, I'm telling you now, Jude, you're going to have to clear this all up when you get in there. James's already thrown you under the bus, so it's only right that you fix the situation."

"Okay, yeah, I have no problem doing that. I'm just not gonna rat on anyone though. I'll fix James's story, and that's all."

"And that's all I expect you to do, Jude. I'm glad we agree on that. Now, you probably already have this part figured out, but there's a pretty good possibility that you won't be coming home today. They'll most likely arrest you on these charges and keep you until you post bail. It's just the way it works, but nothing is for sure."

"But I didn't do anything. Why would they arrest me?"

"Jude, it doesn't matter that you didn't do anything—you were there, and that's all that matters. That's the law. You guys all get the same charges until it's sorted out in the courts.

Most likely, though, we'll just cut a deal with the prosecutor for a much lesser charge, like trespassing. The last thing we want is a felony on your record."

"But do you think I'm gonna do any time?"

"Well, at the most—I'm thinking maybe a year. You'd be out in six months."

I lost the wind in my stomach.

"A year?" I exclaimed.

My face became colorless, and my whole body tensed up. My mom squeezed my hand as tight as she could and put her other hand on my shoulder to keep me in place.

"Jude, these are some damn serious charges—malicious wounding, abduction, firearms, robbery—you're lucky we're not talking about a life sentence here."

"Why abduction? What the hell is that all about?"

"Well, you guys kept those people beyond their will. That's the very definition of the charge."

"What about my medicine, my methadone? Will they give me my medicine?"

"I don't know. We'll have to ask the detective once we get in there. We might as well head in now. Maybe we can start early."

Everyone got up except me. I was glued to the bench, unable to move a muscle.

"Jude, you coming?" my lawyer asked.

My mom leaned over and put her hand on my cheek and whispered into my ear.

"We will make it through this, Son. We are strong. God is with us, and we will make it through. Just submit to Him, and He will guide you through."

She took my hand, and I closed my eyes and willed myself up. There was no escaping my destiny. There was nowhere else to go. For six long years, my parents were always there to throw money at my problems and get me outta jams when I needed them most, but this time around, they were just as helpless as I was.

It wasn't that I feared prison—I feared not having methadone and cigarettes and clean showers and the subtle comforts of freedom. I feared not being able to say goodbye to my father if and when he did die. Prison itself seemed less than scary; it was the circumstances surrounding it that frightened me.

Finally, after walking for what seemed like forever, we reached our destination. There was a heavyset man with a sloped mustache, thinning brown hair, and wire-framed glasses waiting at the end of the corridor.

"That's him," my mom softly said. "He was at the house last night."

We moved closer.

"Are you Detective Prier?" my lawyer asked.

"Yes, yes I am. And you must be—Mr. Gibbons, Jude's lawyer, right?"

"Yes sir, I am. And this is Jude behind me. He's a little nervous as you can expect, but I think we can all agree that he's doing the right thing."

"Absolutely. Jude, as long as you're honest, you don't have anything to worry about," the detective said.

For Lawyer Gibbons and Detective Prier, it was business as usual; they joked and patted each other on the shoulder like old fraternity brothers as my mom and I stood tall behind them stuck in suspense.

Finally, they turned their attention back to me.

"Well, how about it?" my lawyer asked.

"Can my mom come with me?"

"No, no this is gonna be just the three of us, unfortunately," the detective interjected.

I turned to my mom, and we hugged and she told me to be strong.

"Tell Dad I love him, okay? Tell him I'm okay and I'll be home. I love you, Mom."

My mom shook her head, her face pursed up, and she turned around before I could see her cry. Then, she was gone.

I pulled myself together as much as I could and followed my lawyer and the detective into a barren white-walled room with nothing more than a few plastic chairs and a cold aluminum table in the center. The room was bitterly cold and stank of concrete and chemicals. I sat in my respective seat across from the detective, and my lawyer sat to the right of me. Detective Prier switched on a tape recorder, and the interview began.

There wasn't much to tell. There was so much already stacked against me that it didn't make a difference what I said, but I did set the record straight. When the interview concluded, Detective Prier told me that I was being charged with all five felony counts against me and that the courts and the prosecutor would settle everything out when the time came.

"It's time, Jude," he said, pulling a pair of handcuffs outta his belt as two deputies entered the room. "I'm gonna need you to put your hands behind your back now. You can bail out after you see the judge."

"When do you think that might be?" my lawyer asked.

"Well, I don't know, since Jude waited to turn himself in. If you'd have turned yourself in yesterday, you could've seen the judge today and bailed out. Now, it's the weekend, and you won't see a judge until Monday, at the earliest."

"But what about my medicine, my methadone?"

"I'm pretty sure you won't get that. We don't like to condone drug use over here. Just use this as an opportunity to flush yourself out."

"You've gotta be kidding me? Flush myself out?"

I bit my tongue before saying anything else. I put my hands behind my back and felt the cold steel snap around my wrists. I immediately regretted my decision to turn myself in. They had me. It was over.

I was taken to the jail next-door and immediately strip-searched, photographed, swabbed for DNA, and placed in a solitary cell for observation. The whole process took like four hours. They tucked me in my cell for the night and put me in this awful one-piece jumpsuit that was supposedly tear resistant.

"It's to keep you from killing yourself," the guard explained.

"But I never said I was gonna kill myself."

"It doesn't matter. You told the nurse that you were withdrawing. It's protocol to make sure you don't try and harm yourself in the process."

"I wouldn't do that," I pressed further.

"Well, we have numerous inmates who will and who have. We've even had inmates who've broken their own arm or leg or stabbed themselves in the stomach just so they can get their hands on pain meds to make the withdrawals go away. It's amazing what you guys will do for a fix."

"So, I'm just supposed to sit in here and sweat it out?"

"Pretty much. Goodnight."

Yup, it was for sure, I was in hell. Methadone was the reason behind my sobriety, but it was also an unrelenting, bone-penetrating opiate-based drug. In many ways, methadone withdrawal is worse than heroin withdrawal. Actually, it's far worse than heroin withdrawal. For starters, you get the same dose every day like clockwork, so your body becomes accustomed to having just that. With heroin, your dose varies from day to day, so your body isn't as reliant as it is on methadone. Essentially, what I'm trying to say is that I had thirty-six hours before my body went into shock and my organs started tearing apart and crying out for help. Well, thirty-six hours from when I last dosed that morning, so more like less than a day. The clock was ticking.

The only thing that was left to do was pray, and boy, did I ever. I dropped to my knees and prayed like never before.

"God, I sit here before you again in time of need. I cannot go through the pain these people are willing to allow, and I cannot allow the pain they are willing to inflict. I must do something, but I don't know what I can do. Please guide me, God. If not me, then guide this nurse to show compassion to my needs. Guide these officers to show mercy. I have not been a good person, nor have I spoken to you in good times, but if you allow me this chance, I will never forget you. Please help me, God, please!"

I waited for a sign, any sign—but nothing. I sat back against the concrete wall and took in the last few hours of peace before I was, once again, sick in jail. Still, to this day, I can't think of a worse feeling than being dope sick in a confined place without having anything, or anyone, to turn to. Then again, maybe being in there was the answer to my prayers. Maybe that's what I needed to kick the habit once and for all. Maybe sometimes the answer to your prayers is staring you right in the face, but you simply can't see it because you're looking for something else or because you want the easy way out like I always did. Well, there was no easy way out of where I was. God-awful sickness was imminent.

It didn't really hit me until the second night. Up until then, I mostly slept and paced my cell, hoping to come up with some miraculous plan to avoid the fast-approaching illness that was soon to ravage my body like the Plague. I convinced myself that if I cried and screamed enough, someone, somewhere, might actually pull a few strings or bend a few rules to accommodate me. Maybe the mother or father in one of them would come out; maybe they would see my situation as different from all of the others before me. It was all so far-fetched, all so stupid, but thinking kept me busy, and being busy kept me sane. The reality is that there is no place for sympathy or kindness in jail. Everything and everyone around you remind you of that cold-hearted fact. The corrections officers are the ones calling the shots, and if you've ever been to jail or prison, you know how relentless they can be, especially in times of distress. They're not there to hold your hand or wipe your tears away—it's a job to them, and it takes a certain kinda person to do it. I'm not saying they're evil, I'm just saying that whatever compassion they possess is checked at the door. Compassion has no place in jail, especially in the solitary units where mentally anguished inmates fight for attention and do little to hold back their rage.

One such inmate stared at me through his feces-covered window for hours on end without breaking, breathing against the glass with the viciousness of a rabies-infested animal. Above his door hung a sign that served as a warning to all those who dared enter his cell. It read,

"**WARNING: SPITTER, BITER, FIGHTER, FECES THROWER, MENTALY ILL. USE EXTREME CAUTION.**"

Because of him, the entire block smelled like crap, human crap. Most of the other inmates held their shirts over their noses to conceal the smell, but I had that stupid one-piece on that was impossible to contort. Making matters even worse, the A/C never stopped running, not once, so you had all these different smells from all these different cells blowing right into your nose at all times. Then, there was the whole thing with the toilets. I guess they were all connected, or something, because every time someone flushed, even if they were on the complete other side of the block, their crap would rush up into your toilet and you'd hafta flush it back down. But even that was a problem, because you only got a certain number of flushes per hour, and if you wasted them flushing everyone else's crap down your commode, you couldn't flush your own when nature came calling. Lastly, the damn lights never went off—the worst kinda lights too—fluorescents. Needless to say, it was impossible to sleep. Either you slept on your stomach and faced the concrete floor below, or you slept on your back and stared directly into lights all night long.

When the sickness finally took hold of me, I'd gone sleepless and hadn't eaten for an entire day and a half. No way I was gonna eat the slop they were dishing out. Even the best meal of the day, the one in the evening, was atrocious—

unsalted beef slosh and three-day old salad and warm milk and an over-ripened banana. I couldn't even stand to look at the stuff, much less eat it. So I handed my food trays off to the guy in the cell beside me, and he promised to "pay me back the favor" somehow. Anyway, when the withdrawals first hit me, it was only Saturday, and I still had, at least, a whole two days left. Even if I had gotten out on Monday, it wouldn't have been 'til late in the evening because of all the legal paperwork and crap, so I was looking at two days of excruciating pain. It came up on me like a cold at first—sneezes and sniffling and hot flashes. It got progressively worse throughout the night until, by mid-morning, I felt like someone had taken a blender to my insides and scrambled me all up until there was nothing left but a revolting liquid substance that I crapped out every hour or so. I cowered in the corner of my cell, rocking back and forth in the fetal position, blocking as much of the frigid A/C from hitting my sweat-stained clothes as I could.

The only time that I wasn't hurting as badly was when I was using all my energy screaming or crying or puking. It was somewhat of a release, I guess. But it wasn't long before my larynx gave out, and I couldn't scream at all. By the end of Sunday night, I was done. I couldn't move. My body was so sore that it hurt even when I breathed. I simply lay down on the floor, closed my eyes, and cried my eyes out. I didn't even care to make it to the toilet to puke or crap; I just did it on myself, which angered the guards beyond belief, because they'd hafta take me out and clean my cell and give me a fresh set of clothing.

All of a sudden, breaking my own arm or stabbing myself in the stomach with my lunch fork to get meds didn't seem so outlandish after all. There is no doubt in my mind that if I'd have had the strength to do it, I would've. There's nothing, I mean nothing, I wouldn't have done to just end it. I was suffering badly. And all of a sudden, the guy across from me with his feces-covered window didn't seem so out there after all. He seemed normal. It all made perfect sense—he'd simply snapped. That's all. Life just became too overwhelming, and he snapped. But nobody saw that part; all they saw was a deranged man who liked to throw his own excrement and talk to himself. What about the man inside? Surely, he had a story. Surely, he once had dreams and expectations of himself and a family that loved him. Surely, he was once, like—well—like me.

CHAPTER 13

Reckoning

I made it to Monday morning, but barely. The worst part of withdrawal was just starting to hit me, but for the first time—I had something to be hopeful about. My bail hearing was scheduled for noon that day, and I was sure that the judge would take pity on me and let me out in some capacity. Either that, or he'd order a ridiculous bail be paid, and my family would pay it. Both scenarios worked. My lawyer came by to talk to me a couple hours before the hearing.

"How you holding up, Jude?" he asked.

"Not well. How are my parents doing?"

"They're doing okay. I spoke to them this morning, and it looks like your mom and brother are gonna be joining us today in the courtroom."

"What are the chances I'm getting out today?"

"Good."

"Like how good?"

"I'm positive we'll get a reasonable bail set. Then, it's up to you to get bonded out. It just all depends on the judge's mood, ya know?"

"I guess, sure. Look, I gotta get outta here, Mr. Gibbons. I have to."

"We'll get you out, Son. Just hang in there, okay? Is there anything you'd like for me to tell the judge on your behalf? Stuff from your past that could help your cause?"

"Mainly, I just wanna be out there so I can be with my dad. I can't be in here if he dies. And tell him I'm a good kid, just a little lost. I'm done with all that though. I'm turning a new leaf. I'm a different person now. I just need a second— well, a third—chance. But this time, I'm for real."

"Alright, Jude. I'll let him know. Now, make sure you shave up, and try and look presentable. I've brought you some fresh clothes, okay? Let's get it done in there."

"Thanks, Mr. Gibbons. Thanks."

After my lawyer left, a female CO came to my cell and asked me if I wanted to take a shower before my arraignment hearing, and I told her I did. She opened my cell door, and I peeled myself off the ground. We walked a while before coming upon an underground part of the Justice Center where the showers were. She handed me a piece of soap, a towel, a razor, and the clothes my lawyer had dropped off and handed me off to a male CO who was waiting nearby. Together, we walked into the musty shower room, and I stripped down and jumped into the warm stream of water. The water hit me hard, like pieces of glass digging deep into my skin. It'd been a week, or more, since I'd last showered. Chunks of puke and filth and concrete washed off me, and suddenly, I felt human again.

I got dressed and started the long walk across the massive facility to a set of holding cells beneath the courthouse with two COs by my side. They threw me in one of the cells with about ten other guys who smelled like they hadn't showered in years. I was sweating and itching, and my head was so hot that I probably could've lit a cigarette using my hair. I did my best to think about other things, happy things—like getting out, and being home again, and getting dosed at the clinic, and eating a decent meal, and watching TV. The judge finally called out my name after an hour, and I was taken into the courtroom to stand before him.

The bailiff read out my charges, and I looked at the judge's face to try and read his expressions. I looked around the courtroom for my lawyer and saw my mom in the back doing the same, but he was nowhere around. The bastard was sound asleep in the corner. I remember wanting to run over and grab him by the neck and shake every last dime I'd given him outta his pockets, but nevertheless, he got up and made it up to the podium just in time to begin his oratory plea for lenience. He talked about my childhood and my drug problem, my family and my attempt at college. He talked about how I once was a star football player and a standout in the classroom and how I didn't have a record, except for a few minor infractions, and so on. It was all to try and make me look somewhat normal and gain compassion from the judge, and it worked. The judge stopped my lawyer halfway through his speech and set my bail at ten thousand dollars. I nearly fell over where I stood.

Three painfully long hours after my hearing, I was released. My mom forked over the 10 percent to get me out, and I was assigned a bondsman to make sure I made it to my next hearing in a month. Although I was outta jail, I wasn't outta the woods just yet. Any minor infraction—a traffic ticket, even—would've landed me right back in. There was no room to screw up—none at all.

The air outside of the Justice Center couldn't have been fresher. I took what seemed like an endless number of deep breaths to cleanse my lungs of the shit smell that still contaminated them and crawled into the car with my mother. The first place I had her take me when I got outta hell was the methadone clinic. I needed to feel better again so I could concentrate on all the issues before me—Tracy, jail, my dad, and sobriety, to name a few. There was so much I wanted to make right and so much I wanted to undo and say. I'd lost so much valuable time with my father, and he was only months, if not days, away from dying. I felt a sense of urgency that I'd never felt before, like I'd been given a final chance to fix things and there would never be another one like it.

I went home after getting myself together at the clinic and felt brand new. I found my father lying in his usual spot in the basement and didn't waste any time conveying how sorry I was about what'd happened and how hopeful I was about what was happening. Let's just say that he didn't share my enthusiasm.

"Dad, can you ever forgive me? Can you please forgive me?" I begged.

"How many times have I forgiven you, Son?" he replied, barely able to speak. "How many times? A hundred? Two hundred? How many times do we have to do this? I'm dying, Jude. Like it or not, I'm dying. The last thing I ever thought was that I'd be leaving my family like this, in shambles. Your poor mother—how am I supposed to leave her with all of this? Tell me, Son. How?"

"Dad, I'm all better now. Something happened to me in there. Something happened to me, and I know that my words mean nothing right now, but I'm gonna show you. I'm gonna show you how serious I am. You can trust me this time."

My father tilted his head back against his pillow and closed his eyes.

"Okay, Jude. I'm tired now. We'll talk later, okay? I promise."

"Okay, Dad. I love you."

He didn't say anything after that. He was taking so much morphine that he was floating in and outta consciousness and was unable to stay awake for longer than five minutes at a time. The pain was just too unbearable for him to stay awake. There was cancer in almost every part of his body, and on the outside, bedsores and blisters and rashes covered him like a blanket.

I kissed him on the cheek and could feel his cold tears against my lips.

"Please, Dad—don't die. I want you to see me better, okay? Please don't go yet," I whispered into his ear.

He groaned, and I ran to my room panic-stricken. My mom came upstairs after me and did her best to reassure me that everything was gonna be okay for the millionth time.

"How do you do it, Mom? I mean, how are you holding up so well?" I asked, gasping in short breaths in between tears.

"What else can I do? If I don't stay strong, then who will? This is life, Jude."

"But how come you don't hate me, Mom? I've done so much to hurt you guys. Why don't you hate me?"

"Well," she said softly while patting my back. "Well, you're my son. You're my son, and I love you."

That was it for me. My family had held the burden for far too long, and it was time to stand on my own two feet and be the man that my parents had raised me to be. No more drugs. No more caustic friendships. No more regretting. No more testing my boundaries as an addict. No more denying who I was. No more escaping. No more jail. No more numbing my pain. No more. No more. No more.

I started by cleansing my room of every piece of my past. I scraped up every piece of paraphernalia and every ounce and gram and milligram of weed and cocaine from my room and threw it all into the gym bag Tracy had given me back when I first started selling for him. I took the hoodie and jeans I was wearing when we broke into Trent's place and my digital scale and plastic baggies and threw it all in there as well. Lastly, I cleared every last contact and text message and email from my phone and ripped up every last piece of paper in my wallet that had a number on it.

When nightfall came, I grabbed the gym bag with everything in it and threw it in my car. I drove until the road behind my house ended and I was as deep into the woods as I could get and got out. Next, I dug a hole big enough for the bag with my hands, tossed it in, and lit the damn thing on fire, spraying lighter fluid into the hole until the bag was fully engulfed in flames. Smoke billowed into the air, and I couldn't help but smile as my past transformed into a zillion ashes and nothing more. But they were more than just ashes—they were the foundation of what I'd build my new life upon. They'd always be there to remind me of what once was and what would always be: a pile of smoldering ashes just waiting to reignite and burn the whole damn forest down.

I threw water and dirt onto the flames. It was over. I'd burned and destroyed it all—thousands upon thousands of dollars in drugs and every trace of my old life. It was the very definition of a fresh start.

My legal woes weren't over though. Just because I'd decided to be a good boy all of a sudden didn't mean that the things I'd done were gonna just go away. I certainly wish they would've, but the reality was that I was facing an unspeakable amount of time in prison. I did my best to wrap my head around the idea of being in a cage for thirty to fifty years, but it was impossible to come to terms with. The most I could do was stay clean and get healthy and busy and try and prove to the judge and prosecutor that I'd changed and was dedicated to living a life of purity. And I was—it wasn't just for show. I made it my number-one priority to spend as much time with my father as I possibly could in case I did end up going to prison or he ended up passing away like the doctors said he would—both seemed inevitable at that point. And for that same reason, I started decreasing my methadone intake at the clinic against doctor's orders. I'm not sure if it's because he wanted me on that stuff forever, or because he thought I'd end up relapsing again without it, but I didn't care. There were just way too many unknowns for me to be so reliant on something as addictive as methadone. If I'd known for sure that I wasn't going to prison, I probably would've gone a little slower, but I didn't know that for sure, and I wasn't about to risk it. No chance in hell. Not again.

For the next six months, my mother and I went back and forth to the courtroom, each time not knowing if I was gonna be making the return trip home with her. There were continuances, and pre-trial hearings, and motions, and on and on and on until, finally, an agreement was reached—one felony count of abduction with five years' probation and ten thousand dollars in restitution payments made to Trent for hospital bills and court costs. It was the best possible outcome considering the circumstances. It was either that or take the case to trial and place my fate in the hands of a jury of my peers. James had taken that route and was already serving the first year of a ten-year sentence. Tracy and Justin had also decided to take their cases to trial and were consequently sentenced to ten years each. I took the felony and ran.

A week after I was sentenced, my father started letting go. On his final day, the four of us—my mother and brother and sister and me—all gathered around my father's bed in the basement of our home and shared the last few moments of his life with him. The hospice nurse had just left after informing us that, indeed, he was passing and we should prepare for it to happen within the hour. There was nothing left to do but wait, wait and watch my father gasp for his last breaths of air like a fish outta water. We all made sense of the situation by telling ourselves that at least he wouldn't be suffering anymore and he could be in heaven watching over us with the rest of our loved ones. But that meant nothing to me. I was losing my father. I was losing my father, and nothing, absolutely nothing, meant anything to me at that moment but that fact.

My dad was so outta it from all the morphine the nurse had given him that he was conscious but unable to move or talk or even open his eyes. I could tell he was fighting it with everything in him, but the morphine was too strong and he was too weak to overcome it. Every few minutes, he'd yelp out and cry as if he were in pain, but my mom told us that he was just dreaming and that the angels would make sure he didn't suffer too much.

Saying goodbye to my father was the hardest thing I'd ever done in my life. How do you say goodbye to the person who gave you life not once, but twice? We all took turns, starting with my mom and then my brother and then me. When it was my turn to say something, everything that I wanted to say seemed so damn unimportant, and I could only bring myself to mutter a few words.

"It's gonna be okay," I said. "I figured it all out. I won't let you down. Everything is gonna be okay now, Dad."

A lone tear sprung from my father's eye, and I put my hand in his hand and squeezed it to let him know that I wasn't going anywhere. It didn't seem real that I was watching my father pass, and in hindsight, sometimes I wish I never did. I know the last thing he would have wanted was to be remembered like that, but whenever I think of my dad now—it's the only picture I get. Outta all the happy childhood memories and all the proud moments that him and I shared, the only memory I can recall is that one.

As the hour passed and then another, none of us moved from our places around my father, not even to use the bathroom.

A friend of the family had come by, a religious man, to recite the appropriate prayers as my dad faded away. My mother's sisters and their families had also come by to serve as support for my mother in her darkest hour.

And then, at nine in the evening exactly, after all the appropriate prayers had been read out loud and all the last words had been spoken, my father's breathing became heavier and heavier, and I felt him squeeze my hand one last time, and then—he was gone.

I burst out crying and lost myself.

"Dad!" I screamed out. "Dad, please!"

He must've been halfway to the light by then, but upon hearing my cries—he returned for a few more breaths and a loud moan, as if to say one last goodbye.

"No, Son," my mother pleaded with me. "You have to let him go in peace. It's his time."

I couldn't take it anymore. I ran outta the room and buried my face into a sink-full of cold water in the bathroom nearby. I waited a few minutes before coming back out to discover my dad covered from head to toe in a white linen sheet.

"He's gone, Jude. He's gone," my brother announced as he ran up and gave me an overbearing hug.

Just like that, my father, not even sixty years old, was no longer alive. A group of men later came by and removed my dad's body, and my brother and I got to work taking apart the hospital bed he'd been ridden to for weeks. Hospice came and took everything else, and by the morning, it was as if the whole thing hadn't happened.

If ever there was a single good thing that came outta my

father's passing, it was that it made me realize how delicate life was. I mean, there I was—just turning twenty-one—and I'd spent nearly a third of my life putting poison into my body that, at any time, could've killed me. I didn't walk away completely unscathed, of course. I still had a plethora of issues to sort out because of my past decisions, like the fact that I'd started peeing in glass jars because I'd grown so paranoid from years of drug use that I was too scared to get up in the middle of the night and run across the hall to the bathroom. Or the fact that I was still lying just as much as I was when I was using, or the fact that I had to get stuck a hundred times in the arm whenever I went to the doctor to get my blood drawn because my veins were so beaten down from shooting up. And that was only the stuff I knew about—the obvious stuff, the stuff on the surface.

On the one-year anniversary of my father's death, I visited his burial site for the first time since his passing.

"Dad," I whispered. "There's no doubt that without you and Mom, I'd be dead right now, and we'd probably be together. Even when I lost faith in myself, you guys never did, and I don't know how. You are a better person than I could ever be, and I'm sorry for not visiting you—I just figured that if I avoided coming up here, I could just pretend like you were on a really long vacation or something. Silly, huh? Well, I think now I know you're not coming home, and I'm okay with that. I'm gonna do my best to take care of Mom and make you proud of me, okay? I love you, Dad. I love you so, so much. Sweet dreams."

CHAPTER 14

The Call

It'd been almost five years since I'd seen Rachel. I mean, we'd spoken through Facebook and emails and such, but not face to face or over the phone. So when she called and told me she had something important to tell me, I knew it was probably bad news.

"Are you sitting down?" she asked almost immediately.

"Yeah, Rachel. What is it? You're freaking me out."

"Jude, I don't know how else to tell you, but they found Chase with a needle in his arm last night. He's dead, Jude. He's dead. I'm so sorry."

I froze in disbelief. My knees locked up, and I fell to the ground, catching myself with my hands right before I hit the floor.

"They're saying it was heroin. He was with someone, and they just left him to die. I've been struggling so much with it."

I didn't know what to say. I imagined my old friend Chase

lying on the floor with a needle in his arm and blood trickling down his fingers, and I imagined how awful it must've been for him to not be able to scream or pick up the phone and call for help. I imagined how horrified he must've been in the last few hours of his life, wanting so badly to live but being so paralyzed by the drug that all he could do was lie there and slowly pass.

My disbelief immediately turned to anger. I wanted to kill whoever sold him the stuff. I wanted to kill the person who'd left him to die. I hated myself for not being there for him when he needed me most.

"Jude, say something. Please," Rachel cried.

At last, I spoke.

"It's all my fault. I left him. He called me and told me he was better, and I knew he was lying, but I didn't say anything."

"How could you say that? It's nobody's fault, and especially not yours. That's the craziest thing I've ever heard."

Rachel didn't even know the half of it, but she deserved to. She deserved to know what kinda person I was the whole time we were friends in high school and the kinda person I was after high school. She deserved to know, but it wasn't an easy thing to say. It's not every day that you hafta find a way to tell the girl you'd been in love with since tenth grade that you were a heroin addict the whole time you knew her and that you were sneaking off into bathrooms between classes to shoot up. As a matter of fact, I hadn't told anyone my secret since I'd moved to Virginia. Tracy didn't know. My co-workers didn't know. None of the girls I'd dated knew. Not even my friends from St. Louis knew. Just my counselors at the methadone clinic and my family were aware of my past.

But Rachel of all people deserved to know.

"Ray, I have something to tell you too."

"Okay?"

"Well, ummmm, well, I used to get high with Chase. We used to get high together."

"Jude, I know. It's no secret that you used to party and smoke weed and—"

"No, not just weed—heroin. I used to shoot up heroin with Chase almost every day until I went off to school."

Silence—long, miserable silence ensued.

"I haven't spoken those words in a very long time, Rachel. Actually, that's the first time I've ever said that I'm a heroin addict out loud. Now, it's your turn—please say something. Please."

"Jude, it's okay. I love you, and you're an amazing guy, and nothing will ever make me look at you differently, especially not that. So you struggled with addiction? Everyone back here has either been arrested for a DUI or is addicted to something or in jail. Believe me: you're not alone. They're even calling it an epidemic out here, because the heroin thing has gotten so bad. I'm just happy to finally find out what happened to you. You just fell off the face of the earth, ya know?"

"Yeah, well, it's kinda the only way I got clean. My dad brought me up here, and I've been too scared to ever come visit or anything. I guess I'm living somewhat of a fake life out here. Nobody knows about the things I did, and I kinda like it that way. Nobody judges me, ya know?"

I told Rachel everything that night. I opened up to her like I'd never opened up to anyone before. I told her about Tracy and about my dad and college, and I even shared a passage from a journal I'd kept since my father passed with her. I wasn't a journal type of guy, but that damn journal saved my life. I was such an emotional wreck after my father died that I could barely drag myself outta bed. My writing became an outlet, a way for me to vent and eventually come to terms with everything that had happened to me.

Rachel was so blown away by my paper thoughts that she kept asking me to read more and then more, and by the time I was done, the sun was up and we were both in bed.

"Well, I guess it's time for bed," I said, barely able to keep my eyes open anymore. "But can I ask you one last thing?"

"Yeah, of course."

"You remember that letter I wrote you way back in the tenth grade asking you to be my girlfriend?"

She laughed.

"Yeah."

"Well, I kinda downplayed it after you denied me. I know you had a boyfriend at the time, but I really was into you."

"That's funny, because I was into you too. I was just too distracted to see it, I guess. Now that I've lived a bit, my whole outlook on life is different. I don't see things the same anymore."

"I know exactly what you mean."

"I also think that everything happens for a reason, and maybe God was just telling us to wait for the right time."

"Yeah, I agree. Well, I love you, Rachel. Thanks for everything tonight. I'm glad it was you who called and told me about Chase."

"I'm glad it was me too. I love you, Jude. Goodnight."

It's weird, but we'd always said "I love you" to one another, but that night, it was different. When I said it, it felt right, and when she said it, it sounded right. I never believed in the idea of falling in love—not in the normal sense, at least. I guess I'd just given up on the idea altogether ever since I'd had my heart broken in high school by Hailey. Mostly, though—I didn't think I was normal enough for love. I didn't think that a girl like Rachel, a girl who was so beautiful and perfect in every way, could ever see past my past indiscretions and love me for the person I once was—the kid who once had so much going for him and so much to live for and so much to be happy about. I was wrong. Rachel and I fell in love that night—over the phone and in the darkness of my room—over the pages of my past. Surely, Chase had something to do with it. Surely, he was looking down upon us and smiling. We talked every day from that day on and any chance we got. She visited me every other week, and we spent every second learning as much as we could about one another, and she loved me even more the more she knew. I was no longer rebuilding upon the ashes of broken dreams, but creating new dreams and new aspirations and, most importantly, living. I was living.

I asked Rachel to marry me a few months later, and she said yes, and a few months after that, I was headed back to St. Louis to where it had all started. I'd been back a few times since Rachel and I'd gotten engaged, but living there was an entirely different thing. My family was hesitant at first, and so was I. My hometown was in the midst of a heroin epidemic greater than any epidemic before it. Heroin had gotten cheaper and purer and more available since I'd left. It was the worst in the county where dealers had centralized their markets, targeting kids from affluent means who liked to party and were uneducated on the subject of addiction, except for what they'd learned in programs like D.A.R.E. when they were way too young and way too unaffected. And the worst part, the part that turned the problem into an epidemic, was the culture of denial that ran deep in the soccer-mom community. Kids, like me, who nobody would've ever thought in a million years would pick up a habit as vicious as heroin abuse had become the kids most likely to pick up the habit. West County and its surrounding counties were drowning in heroin with no end in sight, and for a former heroin addict in recovery, moving back seemed like suicide.

But St. Louis was my home, and I was confident that I'd never go back using, no matter where I lived. So I left Virginia and landed back where it'd all started less than a decade before. Rachel and I moved in together, and I started working and doing what I could to help plan the wedding. We stayed in most nights and watched movies and ate popcorn and laughed and talked until we fell asleep in one another's arms without an inch to spare between us. It didn't seem real that I'd gotten so lucky. I kept thinking something was gonna happen to mess everything up, but nothing ever did.

We got married on a day that will forever go down as the proudest moment of my life. When I saw Rachel in her wedding dress, I knew that everything was gonna be okay. I knew that it was all for real. I made a vow that day not only to Rachel but also to myself that I'd stop living like I was always gonna fail and start living like I'd never failed, not even once. I was young and I made a mistake, and I paid for that mistake for many, many years. It was time to forgive myself and move on.

I won't lie and say that I don't regret, because I do. I'd take it all back if I could. I hurt a lotta people and squandered a million dreams and wasted a lotta valuable time numbing myself, time that I could've spent with my father. So, yes, I certainly regret putting that first straw up to my nose and that first joint up to my lips, but none of that matters in the end. What matters is that I'm alive. I'm alive, and I appreciate life for what it's worth—for the small things and for the big things and the boring things and the lively things. In the end, I obtained the normalcy that I'd always imagined having—not in the picket-fence, nine-to-five kinda way, but in my own backwards-hat, baggy-jeans kinda way. And that's okay. I realize now that I don't hafta be like everyone else to be happy. I am who I am. I love who I am.

I'm sure that as long as I'm alive, that dark spot on the most vulnerable part of my soul will forever wait for its chance to spring back into my life and ruin me once again. But as long as I'm alive, it'll just hafta keep waiting.

I will never give in. I will never give up. Fuck you heroin. I will never succumb.

Acknowledgments

First, I would like to thank my amazing wife, Rachel. I love you more than words can describe. This book would not have been possible without you and your amazing family—Randy, Gail, Robby and Kristen. I would also like to thank my family—Mom, Dad (I think about you everyday), Zeena, and Noor. Thank you guys for giving me so much when I gave so little. Also, I would like to thank all those who have supported Suburban Junky, Inc. from day one. Thank you Rockwood School District. I am forever grateful for all your help.

Tributes

Travis Henry—I love you, T-Rav.
Joe "Tigger" Divers and Billy Cabral.
Alexander Miele, Bobby Pogue, and Bobby Yahl.
Nathan Ethridge, Michael Alexander Long, Ryan Michael Morris, and Lauren Whittenberg.
John Malaney, Rosemary Strawser, Brad Michael Brinkley, Daniel Matthew Menaugh, and Amy Marie Brown.
-May you all rest in eternal peace.

To all those still struggling with addiction, I am with you every step of the way.

For more information on teenage heroin addiction, visit suburbanjunky.com. For more information on Jude, visit judehassan.com

Made in the USA
Charleston, SC
23 October 2014